The Alexander Technique for Musicians

The Alexander Technique for Musicians

JUDITH KLEINMAN AND
PETER BUCKOKE

methuen | drama
LONDON • NEW YORK • OXFORD • NEW DELHI • SYDNEY

METHUEN DRAMA
Bloomsbury Publishing Plc
50 Bedford Square, London, WC1B 3DP, UK
1385 Broadway, New York, NY 10018, USA

BLOOMSBURY, METHUEN DRAMA and the Methuen Drama logo are trademarks of Bloomsbury Publishing Plc

First published in Great Britain 2013
Reprinted 2014 (three times), 2015, 2016, 2017, 2018, 2019 (twice)

A catalogue record for this book is available from the British Library.

A catalogue record for this book is available from the Library of Congress.

ISBN: PB: 978-1-4081-7458-6
ePDF: 978-1-4081-7684-9
ePub: 978-1-4081-7683-2

Typeset by Newgen Knowledge Works (P) Ltd., Chennai, India
Printed and bound in Great Britain

To find out more about our authors and books visit www.bloomsbury.com and sign up for our newsletters.

CONTENTS

LIST OF FIGURES

ACKNOWLEDGEMENTS

We would like to thank all our Alexander teachers, colleagues and friends who have helped us on the way to writing this book and the Musician/Alexander teachers from the training schools, who have contributed some of the 'Student quotes'.

A very large thank you must go to Paul Chapman and Lori Schiff for their thorough reading of our script and their extremely useful suggestions of how to improve our book.

The diagrams are the excellent work of David Ashby.

The photo of Ruairi working with children (Chapter 18: Teacher–pupil relationships), on the RCM outreach programme, was provided by Sheila Burnett.

Thanks go to Michael Deason-Barrow, Head of the Tonalis Institute, for letting us use his description of the 'Roles of the Larynx'.

The two (video) images of the Schubert Ensemble were provided by Rob Hardcastle.

Our two sons

The photos are mostly the work of Abe who not only took the photos but also made the multi-image plates that give the sense of movement that is vital in this work. Harry gave us advice on how to organize and present the script. Harry and Abe are both in several of the photos. We would like to thank them both for their enthusiasm and support throughout the process of writing this book.

RCM

We are very grateful to the staff at the Royal College of Music, who have supported us through the development of the Alexander courses over the past 20 years. Special thanks go to Dr Elisabeth Cook (Head of Academic Development and Undergraduate Programmes) who has been with us for every step of the journey. Many thanks also go to Dr Amanda Glauert (Director of Programmes and Research) for her enthusiastic support and the quote about her personal experience of the Technique. Thanks also to David Harpham (Registry Officer) who has given us a taste of his personal experience of the Technique to include in the book.

The biggest debt of gratitude goes to the students at the Royal College of Music. We have observed their progress over the years and developed courses and ways of teaching from the interactive experience of sharing the Alexander Technique with these talented and highly intelligent musicians. Particular thanks go to the students who have given us permission to quote them and use photos of them in our book.

FOREWORD

Since the 1950s, the Royal College of Music has been leading the music world in the use of the Alexander Technique in the training of the music students from countries throughout the globe. The Technique is a facilitator in the learning process. The musician's job is a craft that requires excellent coordination and an art that requires creativity and spontaneity. These aspects of performance are addressed with clear and practical guidance in The Alexander Technique for Musicians. The Alexander department at the RCM collaborates with our Centre for Performing Science on research and development. This book is evidence of over 20 years of research by our Alexander teachers, looking at how to best demonstrate and explain the Technique to musicians.

This book has been written with the performing musician in mind. It sets out a very clear explanation of the basics of the Alexander Technique and makes connections that will be useful for players of all instruments. There are photos of many College students that have taken part in Alexander courses and quotes from students that give a sense of just how useful the technique can be for aspiring musicians.

The authors, Judith Kleinman and Peter Buckoke, have the advantage of being highly accomplished and successful performing musicians, working in the London music scene. They have decades of experience teaching the Alexander Technique to musicians at the RCM. Many of their students have taken the technique deeply into their instrumental or vocal technique as well as their approach to performance. It is often our alumni that developed a keen interest in the Alexander Technique that are making the most impressive strides on the professional concert platforms and performing at the highest level in international competitions.

I have every confidence this will become a standard work that will be considered essential reading by all musicians, not only students, who are interested in exploring the potential of the Alexander Technique in relation to practice and performance.

Professor Colin Lawson
Director of the Royal College of Music, London

PART ONE

Prelude

CHAPTER ONE

Why might a musician use the Alexander Technique?

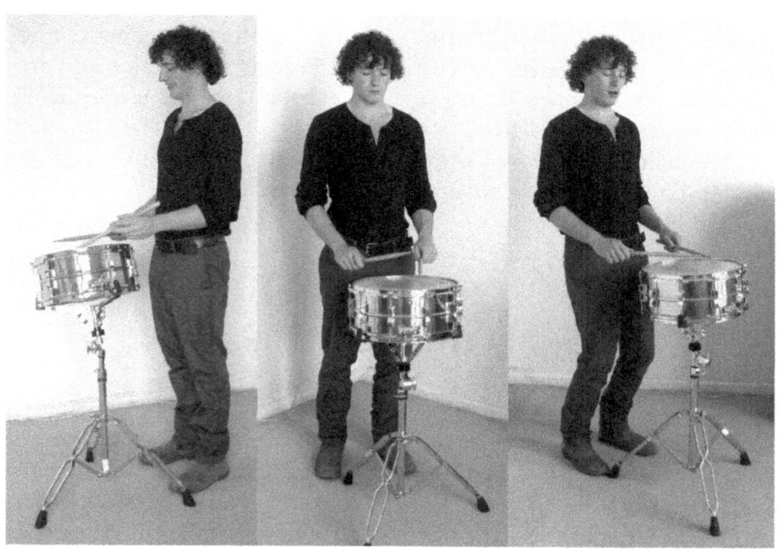

To say a musician plays with his hands is like saying a runner runs with his feet![1]

---

[1]Yosuke Riley Chatmaleerat, pianist.

Health involves many things at many levels but full health is impossible unless we can maintain a balanced equilibrium in the face of forces which tend to disturb us.[2]

You could ask why humans might use the Alexander Technique in relation to any activity. One way of looking at this is to notice that some people find it easy to excel in their chosen field without any knowledge of the Alexander Technique. In fact, there are many musicians who are superbly coordinated without having learnt the Technique, however the majority of musicians do not have their best coordination available to them all of the time. It is quite often the case that a musician will have experienced moments of brilliance that convince them that they can play better than they do some or most of the time. Those glimpses, of achieving something like their potential, keep them practising hour after hour in the search of reliable coordination in their playing in general and performances in particular. Musicians are keen to practice and are expecting to learn by doing so. The Alexander Technique helps you to 'learn how to learn'.

The technique is based on principles that help you to establish reliable coordination in your life and music making, so you are more likely to be able to do what you want to do in the way that you choose.

Highly trained athletes

Musicians have to train in a similar way to Olympic athletes. We may not need the heart and lung development of some athletes but we have to train various groups of muscles to even greater fitness and finesse than many sportsmen and women. We devote thousands of hours to developing our skills and we can easily feel under pressure when performing, just like athletes.

---

[2]Wilfred Barlow, *The Alexander Principle*, Arrow Books, London, 1984, p. 47.

Talent versus skill

There is a generally held belief that 'talent' makes the difference between just being able to learn the sport or the instrument and reaching the higher levels of performance. Talent is all about doing what is required at the given moment; some musicians have those skills in place intuitively. The Alexander Technique helps you develop the way the mind and body connect, communicate and function in all activities. You could say, it develops your talent by working on the skills that the 'talented' have left in place, because they have not interfered with their coordination.

Modern life

Modern daily life includes sitting in front of computers, using the mobile, watching the TV, all of which can find us disengaging from our body and thinking only of the content on the screen in front of us – life has become more sedentary. We may think of relaxation in terms of collapsing on the sofa – on the other hand, when we come to play our instrument we have the idea of sitting or standing up straight (neither of them ideal). Alexander Technique helps us realize there is a connection between our Use in daily life and our music making.

Comfort and discomfort

The lifting, carrying and playing of a musical instrument often involves adopting challenging positions and movements. We might have to sit on an unsuitable chair for 6 hours or more in a day in a cramped space. We might have to travel for hours squeezed into an economy airline seat and then have to perform. The player moves to get a sound from the instrument and the movements can be comfortable or uncomfortable. If the early stages of learning a new instrument include discomfort, a critical situation has been reached. If at that point the musician decides that the discomfort is not acceptable and seeks a solution, the chances are that the learning will go on rapidly in a good direction. If the student musician puts up with discomfort or pain, the journey ahead will be going in the wrong direction. The unfortunate problem, or human challenge, is that we can easily override the discomfort on a tide of enthusiasm for the music or a passionate desire to play the instrument. Some musicians are so keen to play they screen out their sense of quality of movement that might avoid the discomfort in the first place.

'There is no gain without pain'

The problem with that maxim is that the gain will be for the companies that make painkillers and for osteopaths rather than the musician.

Before the pain stage has been reached we have gone through poor coordination, awkwardness and increasing discomfort. If we can reverse the process we reduce the pain to discomfort to comfort and improve coordination along the way. There is almost always unnecessary tension involved in the negative pattern and there is, unfortunately, a corresponding reduction in sensitivity or sensation experienced through the body's nervous system. So to state the situation briefly, 'tension reduces sensation'. We learn to notice attitude, extra tension, loss of balance and freedom. Applying Alexander's principles puts us back in the more reliable control of our reflex systems. One of the skills we learn when we study this technique is how to stop and recover.

Pain as a stimulus (Peter's story)

Often musicians come to Alexander work through the 'discomfort and pain' route. I am an example. Initially I was perfectly happy to use the technique to 'just get out of pain'. When I got out of pain, by studying the Alexander Technique, I enjoyed playing, practising and performing much more. I started to see the musical potential of the principles as a by-product of the pain-relieving journey I was taking. Looking back, I am glad I had pain as a stimulus; I had to change! The musical pay-off was very exciting. I changed my expectations of what I might achieve musically and have been changing them ever since. I realized you don't have to react automatically on the basis of your feelings all the time; you can make conscious decisions about interpretation and creativity. Thinking back, I can remember being in rehearsals and not being open to musical suggestions from colleagues or conductors because I felt they were wrong; after Alexander lessons I became a more flexible musician because I realized I could choose my behaviour consciously.

A brief look at musical habit

To briefly consider matters musical; the Alexander Technique looks at habit. Do we respond habitually in musical situations? Do we always play the same short notes when there are dots on them? Do we always produce the same sound in legato tunes? Do we respond to 'A' major in a predictable way? Do we rush in fast music or when there is a crescendo in the part? Is our habit to play quietly in the same old way when our solo line in a sonata changes to an accompaniment? Have we developed habitual responses that stifle creativity and spontaneity? To be spontaneous and creative we have to avoid habitual, automatic playing. Alexander Technique can liberate the musician from habit and free up their musicianship.

Practice

Alexander work has a lot to offer in the practice room. We look at the structure of our time spent there, including playing and not playing. We consider the use of semi-supine position as a practice tool, often combined with the use of imagination. We explore the efficient development of instrumental technique and preparation of pieces for performance. We question our use of repetition and qualities that we can bring to it. We consider the influence of our balance, breathing, seeing and hearing on our playing. We look at our attitude and how to deal with our expectations of our practice. We develop a connection between the way we use our mind and body in relation to our instrument and developing musical responses. We endeavour to open our mind to enjoying ourselves and maintaining comfort and health while engaging in this essential part of being a musician.

Performance

The Alexander Technique can help us to see the differences between practice and performance. We develop our ability to communicate with our colleagues and the audience. As consciousness of our psychophysical responses to playing and performing develop, we improve our ability to express our genuine relationship with the music.

Performance anxiety

Musicians have complex demands on them and many of us experience performance anxiety. Some players seem to have no problem with performing and stay sanguine when other players are feeling stressed.

The way Alexander saw this situation was simply that we are experiencing our 'habitual response to the stimulus'. I am sure we all find it possible to say or think, 'This is a big concert, no wonder I am feeling shaky!' However, we can probably agree that the complex music or the 'high profile recital' is not the problem; the problem is our response to the situation. When you feel stressed before a concert, you are (presumably) not choosing that response. The recognition and understanding of this is the start of a road to recovery. If you develop a deep understanding of the Alexander Technique, you can find a solution to performance anxiety.

Look after yourself for more than one reason

No musician would damage their instrument on a daily basis and expect it to work well but some of us misuse our body and apparently expect it to carry on producing good results for a lifetime. Some performers have continued to perform at the highest level of the profession for many decades. Rubenstein, Casals, Horowitz and Heifitz spring to mind. Every one of them had great Use. Studying the Alexander Technique can improve our Use and prepare us for a long, successful and comfortable career.

Perhaps the biggest gift of the Alexander Technique is how it allows us to become deeply present and involved in the moment of making music.

Student quotes

Many musicians are not aware that when they come to play their instrument, they are actually using two instruments. Their Self is the primary instrument and the musical instrument is the secondary one. If one is ever to find full pleasure and comfort with playing one's secondary instrument, one's primary instrument must be working in a way which allows that.

Ashok Klouda, cellist

The most crucial change in my thinking that the Alexander Technique has influenced is the awareness of the fact that I am able to take responsibility for my body and mind. It is my decision how I treat my body, how I practise, how I deal with stressful times and how I respond to physical pain or psychological pressure.

Anna Eichholz, violinist

CHAPTER TWO

How to use this book

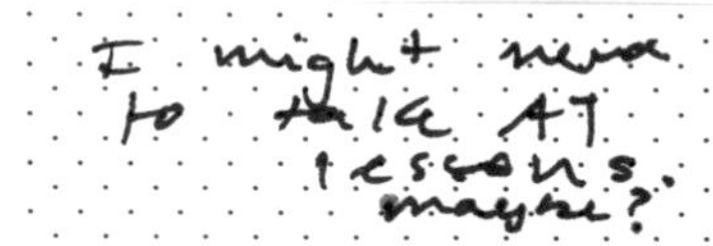

We have written this book for musicians who are receiving Alexander lessons. The book will also be useful if you are not having lessons, though we encourage you to have the hands-on experience of Alexander lessons if you can. Alexander work is oriented to thinking about what you are doing while you are doing it. The experience of interacting with a teacher helps you understand the approach to improved use of the mind and body that is potentially mystifying if you only read about it in a book.

The writing does not avoid reiteration of key points. It will be productive to read the book from cover to cover but it has been written and organized in a way that makes it easy to dip into different aspects of the Technique and musicianship, chapter by chapter. If you have not heard an account of how Alexander developed his Principles we strongly recommend that you read Chapter 3: 'Alexander's discoveries and the development of his ideas'. We also encourage you to read Part Two of the book, 'The fundamentals', first because a familiarity with the basic ideas will help you with all the other chapters. If you are unfamiliar with any of the Alexander terms that we use, you will find a brief explanation in the 'Glossary' at the back of the book.

The intention of our book is to throw light on an Alexander approach to life and music, demystify ideas that might start by being confusing, and to make the principles of the Technique more easily understood. If your Alexander teacher mentions something new to you, we hope you will find references to it in this book. Sometimes, in a lesson, you might simply have the experience of 'hands on' Alexander work with little verbal explanation, this often works at a deep level.

Some Alexander teachers are musicians but most are not. We have gained some of our greatest insights into playing from Alexander teachers who are non-musicians. If your Alexander teacher is not a musician you might find that the musical connections we make in this book help by backing up what your teacher is covering. When you have understood the Alexander principles and can apply them to an activity, that newly acquired skill is transferable to all other activities including playing your instrument or singing.

We have written this text with the musician in mind, the musician who is looking to develop their musical skills in general and specific ways by understanding and applying the Alexander Technique to practice and performance.

We have chosen the photos because they suggest light connected energy, rather than demonstrating approved 'postures' or 'being perfect'. There is always a message relating to freedom of movement, coordination and balance behind the pictures.

We have drawn on inspirational published sources – F. M. Alexander being the most important; Wilfred Barlow whose work and research at the Royal College of Music inspired the University level teaching of the Technique to musicians and Frank Pierce Jones, a scientist/Alexander teacher who researched the Technique in relation to musicians. We include brief biographies (at the back of the book) to put these figures in historical perspective, we have also described the development of the teaching of the Technique at the RCM from Dr Barlow's ground breaking experiment in the 1950s to the present day. You will find a comprehensive bibliography of significantly influential published material that we encourage you to delve into if you are fired up with enthusiasm for this endlessly fascinating approach to life in general and playing music in particular. If you are looking for an Alexander teacher or a teacher training school we have included contact details for the UK and International Alexander societies (p. 299).

The driving force behind our writing of The Alexander Technique for Musicians is our experience of teaching the thousands of music students who have passed through our hands over the past 20 years at London's Royal College of Music. The courses we run and the way we teach are constantly evolving under the influence of interaction with, and feedback from, these intelligent, talented and often delightful young musicians. You will see brief quotes in most of the chapters, some from written work by our students, some from musician/Alexander teachers whom we have taught over the past few years.

CHAPTER THREE

F. M. Alexander's discoveries and the development of his ideas

F. M. Alexander © 2013 The Society of Teachers of the Alexander Technique, London

Alexander's Technique developed over a number of years, as he came to terms with his problems on stage, performing as an actor and reciter. He made fundamental discoveries that were the solution to his vocal problems. He realized the discoveries were useful in many situations and the ideas developed into his Principles. These Principles are what we now know as the Alexander Technique. We can all relate to the unfolding of his story and to a certain extent we all have to do what he did, if we want to develop reliability and confidence in performance.

Alexander was showing great promise as an actor but he was developing problems with his voice. His vocal problems arrived at crisis point in his early twenties, when his career was taking off. Even though he had taken acting and elocution lessons from eminent teachers, he was developing hoarseness in performances so he consulted a doctor. His doctor examined him, found no pathology and so assured him that he had simply overused his voice and advised rest. Alexander's voice was fine at the start of his next performance but he was soon struggling and by the end of the show he could hardly speak. He was very anxious about his future prospects.

He thought about his situation and reasoned that he must be doing something in performance that was straining his voice, something that he did not do at other times. He returned to the doctor for his professional opinion; he asked the doctor to watch him as he spoke and recited, with a view to identifying what he was doing. The doctor said a very significant thing to him, 'I cannot see the problem.' Alexander accepted that he was creating his vocal problem by doing something that appeared normal, even to a medically trained expert. The doctor admitted that he could help Alexander no further.

Alexander went home with the intention of solving the problem with self-observation, mirrors and experimentation. At first, like the doctor, he could see nothing unusual. (It is important for musicians to acknowledge that we might find it difficult to see the negative habits that are influencing our playing.) Alexander began to notice some things that he was doing, like tensing his feet on the floor. After some time he began to see he had a tendency to shorten the muscles in the back of his neck when he was reciting. (This is an expression of stress or fear, also known as part of the 'startle pattern'.) It took some time but he found that on a temporary basis he could prevent the shortening of the neck muscles that pulled his head back and down in relation to his spine. He noticed that when he managed to avoid pulling his head back and down his voice became less strained and his breathing became freer. He had discovered the first piece in his Technique's jigsaw, the Primary Control. The way the head relates to the spine has an effect on coordination in general but at this point he was seeing the particular effect on his vocal mechanism. As he continued working in this way his voice became more reliable and he saw clearly that the way he used his body affected the way it functioned – this became central in his thinking and one of his Principles – 'Use Affects Functioning'.

He found the picture was more complex. He noticed that reorganizing his head Forward and Up made him feel lighter and more energized. However, if he got deeply 'involved' in his recitation, he would go back to habit, which he noticed by now also included lifting his chest and narrowing his back, restricting his breathing and putting pressure on his larynx. This crystallized into another Principle, Psychophysical Unity; the mind, body and emotions are continuously affecting each other. He needed to find a way for his head to go Forward and Up, for his back to lengthen and widen and his larynx to remain poised and flexible, including when he was deeply involved in reciting. He noticed that the body did not work in sections but as a whole mind–body unity. He found it did not work to concentrate on small sections of his body, for example, just his vocal organs. He saw clearly that his new way of working was most effective when he considered his Whole Self.

Sometimes, to his surprise, he noticed in the mirrors that he was not doing what he felt he was doing. This was a very significant discovery and an essential part of his understanding of his problem. By now he had noticed that he had the same pattern of tension in his everyday speech as well as his performing voice. He could not rely on the feedback from his sensory nervous system to tell him what he was doing. His understanding of this condition developed into another Principle of the Technique, Faulty Sensory Perception. (We all have the potential for Unreliable Sensory Perception even if it is only things like, thinking we are hearing a unison when it is actually an octave.) He decided that he was more likely to see the truth in the mirror than sense it through his feelings.

He noticed, in the mirror, that his determination to do something new was not enough to effectively make the change because his old habit was stronger than his new intention. (Most of us know it can be difficult to change a habit!) He realized that he had to be very clear about the pattern he needed to stop. This he saw as a corner stone of his Technique – he called it Inhibition. He found the stopping of the old pattern had to be an on-going priority, until the old habit had been weakened enough to make the new pattern available without the interference from the old. When he managed to put Inhibition in place he found he was making significant progress.

This realization, that determination or trying hard to do something different did not achieve the goal he was looking for, led him to consider the influence of his emotional state and his attitude to speaking. He realized that he could not choose his emotional state but he could choose his thinking and that had a huge effect on his feelings and coordination. This took form in his concept of End-gaining, which he saw as an impatience to achieve a result directly. His alternative strategy was to work out the best means that would eventually take him to his intended goal.

Alexander discovered a way of speeding up the process of change. This new idea, he called Direction. He had discovered that it was no good to push his head Forward and Up – he needed to somehow access the reflex that exists in us to do exactly that. We all had this coordination as young children and some people have not lost it. He found if he directed movement or release, wishing it to happen, this had a subtle effect that speeded up change. So now he had twin allies in Inhibition and Direction both working against his negative habits.

He found it important not to 'try hard to make change happen', a negative approach he described as 'Doing'. Instead, he used Inhibition and Direction to encourage his head to balance and was curious to notice any change, he referred to his new (just thinking) approach as 'Non-doing'. He was allowing the changes to happen rather than forcing the issue. He found this worked on a subtle reflex level. He was working out the Means-whereby he might best achieve his goal. He found, if he directed throughout the activity, his coordination and breathing improved and his sensory awareness became more reliable. His movement became full of poise and lightness, his acting was admired, he became known for his resonant voice. He found himself in great demand as an actor and teacher. His journey included self-acceptance on the path to self-development. He had to recognize deeply ingrained habits and approach their change with patience and perseverance. This approach helps a musician develop the myriad skills that they need to become an inspired, creative performer.

Summary

He developed the Principles

- Use Affects Functioning
- Psychophysical Unity
- Faulty Sensory Perception
- Recognition of Habit
- Primary Control
- Inhibition
- Direction

Alexander came to a clear understanding of some basic truths about being human. He found a way to help us to choose how we react to whatever happens in our lives, consciously rather than automatically. This helps us develop the possibility of being present, creative and spontaneous when we might have otherwise have lived, practised and performed habitually. His work helps us to deal with our fears and find flexibility in mind and body – what every musician is looking for.

PART TWO

The fundamentals

CHAPTER FOUR

Habit in the learning process

Habits are not an 'untied bundle' of isolated acts. They interact with one another and together make up an integrated whole. Whether or not a particular habit is manifest, it is always operative and contributes to character and personality.[1]

F. P. Jones

Babies learn fast

As babies we learn about interactions with things and people, without instruction. We experiment and repeat anything that is fun or satisfying. In those early days, there is no formal instruction but we are constantly learning. How much are we affected by our family and friends? Do we learn breathing patterns from our parents? How many of our inherited characteristics are 'genetic' and how many copied patterns of response? How often do we see or hear mannerisms of the parent or grandparent in the child or grandchild? We learn how to speak our first language from our parents and we tend to have their way of speaking and using language.

---

[1]F. P. Jones, *Freedom to Change*, Mouritz, London, 2003, p. 100.

Children learn easily

Aki is demonstrating that for him it is a simple matter to put a violin under his chin without disturbing his balancing system.

He is well connected with the ground; his shoulders are free from unnecessary tension.

He is learning very efficiently and it is no surprise to hear him say that he really enjoys playing.

Children learn easily

When we look at the way children develop in their first few years we notice that learning is impressively rapid and apparently easy. If a parent has to be away from their child for a few days, they will notice a big change when they return. New activities are learnt and the way of doing them changes easily as they develop their skill and coordination, they don't seem to get stuck in 'habit'. Young children are happy to get things wrong and find it easy to have another go with no idea of negativity. When you see a child experimenting with walking, they keep on having another go and usually look very happy while they are doing it. As we get older and experience judgemental pressure to get things right (possibly at school) the rate of learning seems to slow down. Maybe, being happy to get things 'wrong' is a path to rapid learning.

> *I feel it in a changed attitude toward failure which doesn't feel like a setback or the writing on the wall, but like a path forward.*[2]

---

[2]Daniel Coyle, *The Talent Code*, Arrow Books, New York, 2010, p. 217.

- As children we learn easily
- Non-judgemental support encourages easy learning

A definition of habit

A habit is a pattern of behaviour that has been developed in the past, often consciously, which tends to get repeated automatically in similar circumstances, more or less subconsciously. It is possible to bring most habits into the conscious realm to have a look at them. It can be difficult or very difficult to change habits and more difficult if we don't really want to change, but it is possible to change habits.

- Alexander work is a means of recognizing and changing habits.

Habits feel good

Alexander referred to the way someone uses their mind and body as their Use.

The way we use our mind and body affects the way they function, both now and, because of the power of habit, in the future. We need to be aware of the strength of habit as well as its potential usefulness. If we accept, as Alexander discovered, that our sensory feedback is not necessarily reliable (what he called 'Faulty Sensory Awareness'), we can appreciate that some of our habits may not be as good as they feel, they may even be seriously damaging, for example, smoking. There is something secure about familiarity and most of us search for familiar feelings of security; if that secure feeling comes from a negative pattern, we will have trouble recognizing and changing it. We have probably all tried to change habits and know how hard that can be, for example, changing the way we hold our instrument or the way we stand, or sit on a chair.

Three examples of standing and sitting. From left to right – overarched, balanced and slumped. Overarching involves unnecessary effort and the extra tension creates pressure throughout the body. Slumping involves a lack of necessary tension and also creates pressure throughout the body. Balanced Use acknowledges the design of the body and makes appropriate use of the skeletal structure with appropriate muscular tension and so the minimum pressure throughout the body.

Free will

Maybe free will starts at the 'light-bulb moment' when we first realize we are having a chance to choose one course of action over another in our life. This is when we start developing our capacity to inhibit an automatic or impulsive approach to life. Maybe, as a child, we experienced the possibility of eating a treat now or saving it until later. We can then develop our experience of choice, whenever we are prepared to acknowledge to ourselves that we don't have to do what 'we feel like doing' impulsively; or indeed, what we imagine 'we should do'. That knowledge is precious knowledge indeed.

- Habits are usually subconscious
- Habits feel familiar and reassuring
- Our feelings can be unreliable
- Free will involves conscious choice

Habit and skill

The link between habit and skill is a very close one. When learning a new skill, for example, playing a musical instrument, riding a bike, speaking a foreign language, we develop patterns of behaviour that are apparently 'the right ones' – we are successfully playing, riding or speaking! We may have a teacher who is telling us that we are doing well and encouraging us to continue. The consciously learnt element of the skill becomes second nature and we think less and less about the various new elements of the skill and there we are; we have a collection of habits that we can describe as a new skill.

If we are learning a new language, in an ideal linguistic world we have learnt nothing but the correct words with an authentic style of delivery that makes it possible to communicate brilliantly in our chosen new language. Most likely, however, we have some less than perfect habits in the new language that could stay there for years. Getting by successfully in the language might limit improvement; it depends on our motivation. This is the same for riding the bicycle and playing the musical instrument. Our attitude to improving a skill that is already 'well developed and useful' could be seen as part of our 'character'. Is our character a collection of patterns of behaviour that we have developed in the past and tend to repeat automatically in similar circumstances? If it is, we are back with habit.

If we are not constantly reviewing how we are doing what we are doing while we are doing it, we will not continue to refine of our skills. Musicians are involved in skills that can be infinitely refined. We can continuously develop the Use of the mind and body and expand our field of attention to improve our playing, our interaction with our colleagues and our communication with the audience.

Essential habits

It seems that developing habits is a vital part of developing as a human. We need to have thousands of automatic responses that can deal with most of our everyday lives.

The risk is that we *only* respond on that automatic level and get stuck in the way we do things, we become predictable or a stereotypical character; we limit ourselves when we get stuck like this. We might hear someone say, 'That's the way I do it' or 'I am always anxious before concerts.'

Alexander noticed that it was not just his coordination that was stuck in a habit – his attitude of mind towards what he was doing was stuck too. His genius allowed him to realize this. He saw he needed to work on both at the same time. This is how he arrived at his realization of 'psychophysical unity' (the mind and body continuously affect each other).

A few questions

- Do you have a habit of repeating passages when you practise them? If you do repeat them, do you really consider why you are doing that?

- Do you have a habit of mental chatter, while you are practising?
- Do you have a habit of rushing to unpack your instrument and start playing as soon as possible?
- Is it your habit to set short-term goals and ignore your long-term development?
- Is your habit an obsession with the results rather than the way to achieve the results?
- Is your habit to screen out your body's feedback?
- Is your habit to feel competitive?
- Do you have a habit of noticing other people's negative habits?
- Is your habit to notice the negative things about your playing rather than the positive things?
- Do you have a habit of thinking that getting things wrong is a failure, rather than a path of learning?
- Is your habit to enjoy your playing?

The trick seems to be to review our habits and check that we want to recommit to them, as 'the best we can come up with in the present circumstances', if not, we need to try something new! This opens the door to constantly developing our language, piano playing or safe cycling, throughout our life.

Deeper learning

Alexander's approach to learning is psychophysical. Are you aware of your body when you are learning music or are you just learning in your mind? Are you aware of your vision and your breathing? Are you aware of your balance? It is possible to play a musical instrument more or less subconsciously, deep in habit. That lack of awareness of what you are doing slows down the learning process.

It is easy to be very committed to learning a musical instrument, so committed that we can ignore messages from our body about comfort and coordination. That leaves us at the mercy of our habits. If you are so set on playing the notes that you ignore discomfort or pain, you are not doing yourself a favour. In fact, you will play your instrument better if you listen to your body's responses to how you are doing what you are doing. A comfortable wide-awake body is being used well and it will learn music more easily. We benefit from the feedback from our senses while we are playing. The more awake we are the more feedback we get.

Emotional responses

Our emotional response to the music is a vital part of learning how to play it. The reason that most music exists is to communicate its emotional content. From the start of learning a new piece, we can include musical/emotional responses. We might have to remember that the emotional or musical content of the piece is expressed through necessary playing movements. Our musicality and our movements can become habitual; however, our thinking and awareness can keep us spontaneous.

It is good to notice if we have a physical habit to go with a certain type of playing, for example, when we are playing pianissimo, we might have a mannerism to show that we are playing pianissimo.

We can get stuck in habitual emotional responses to music as much as we can in our daily lives. Some people have the habit of putting themselves under a lot of pressure to 'get everything right', all of the time. Alexander considered the emotional self as part of the psychophysical whole.

We can also get stuck in a particular musical style. An understanding of style helps us to play music from different centuries or countries differently but that is not the end of the story, we still need flexible emotional responses, whatever the style.

It is interesting to consider if we have any choice in our musical responses. Some musicians sound the same whatever they are playing. Do we play according to our habitual emotional responses to music, or can we be flexible? We can find choice, and so spontaneity, if we are aware of other possibilities. It is very useful to discuss and share musical ideas with other musicians, to test and expand our musical options. Playing with inspiring musicians expands our musical possibilities if we are truly present while we are playing. Openness in our mind, body and emotional self will make every musical interaction a potential learning experience.

- There is a strong link between habit and skill
- Our emotional and musical responses can be habitual
- If we are aware of the power of habit we become more flexible

Work on one or two habits at a time

The Alexander Technique is concerned with looking into how we do what we do while we are doing it. We identify habits and make reasoned assessments of them. When we find habits that need our attention, it is best to have one or two that are our priority for the present. That way the burden of the challenge is reasonable. If we try to change too many habits at the same time we can lose heart as our brain overheats.

Don't be too tough on yourself

Don't beat yourself up about your negative habits. You have often developed them for a reason; even if you have decided something is not good now it might well have been a good idea at the time. Self-acceptance is an important part of self-development. Being able to stand back and observe what is going on will be easier if you make your observations with compassion. Alexander noticed that negative habits often involve trying too hard to get results, which is another way of being tough on yourself. The technique creates a framework for recognizing and then reducing or avoiding that 'trying too hard'.

Finding habits using semi-supine

If we lie down in semi-supine, we often notice pockets of tension in parts of our body. We can enlist the help of gravity and think Directions to release the extra tensions. If we lie down the following day and find the same tensions, we can decide to work out how and when we create the patterns. When we leave semi-supine, it is a rich opportunity to notice the negative patterns as they try to re-establish themselves. Well-constructed Directions designed to contradict the habits work powerfully in our favour.

Using video

We can make use of modern technology to help in the search for our negative habits. If you have a smart phone, you can probably video your practice. The practice continues as you watch the play back. Reflections in mirrors or shop windows can give moments of insight too. It is good to take 'recognition of habit' into everyday life.

We bring our daily Use into our playing

You cannot expect to use yourself one way in daily life and another way when you play your instrument. If you try to 'put your posture right' for playing, you will have limited success. If we develop expanding, reflex, balanced Use in everyday activities, it will be there for us when we are playing as well. The way that you stand or sit when you are not playing informs the way you stand or sit when you are; that is the power of habit!

- Habit is part of being human.
- Instrumental technique is a collection of habits
- Habits are necessary
- Habits can get in the way of our development
- We can use video to see and hear our habits

- Awareness of the power of habit will facilitate clear thinking
- Inhibition of habit makes it possible to be flexible and spontaneous

Student quotes

During an observation lesson last term, in which I played the piano, it was pointed out to me that I have a tendency to pull in my lower spine when I play. To address this habitual response I began to realise other times in my day when exactly the same response would occur; washing the dishes, lifting something heavy, talking to someone who intimidated me – in all of these situations I noticed myself going through the same pattern of responses – this had become my very own personalised startle pattern.

Susanna Macrae, pianist

For a singer perhaps more than for instrumentalists, the body is the instrument, and regardless of all the goodwill and practice in the world, distortions in the body will ultimately lead to distortions in the voice. Practice, in fact, can be a fairly counteractive measure, if all we are doing is reinforcing a faulty habit over and over again.

Phoebe Haines, singer

CHAPTER FIVE

The Primary Control

When the Primary Control is functioning as it should, it is sensed as an integrating force that preserves freedom of movement through the system so that energy can be directed to the place where it is wanted without developing strain either there or elsewhere.[1]

F. P. Jones

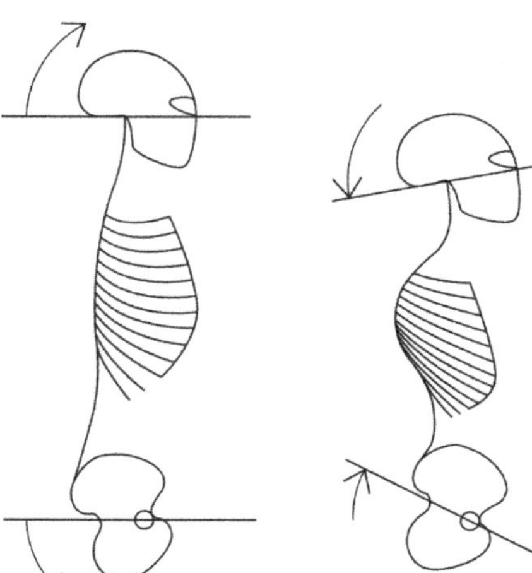

Primary Control

The quality of freedom in the Primary Control affects the whole body.

The balance of the head influences the spine, the ribcage and the pelvis.

[1]F. P. Jones, *Awareness Freedom and Muscular Control*, Sheldrake Press, London, 1968, p. 13.

The term Primary Control refers to the relationship between the head and the rest of the body. The head balances on the top of the spine. (This joint might be higher than you think.) Our head is rather heavy (roughly – 5 kilograms) and if it is not in balance we will experience tension, pressure or heaviness. This affects our breathing, coordination and sense of well-being. If we tend to worry, lack confidence or suffer anxiety, these attitudes will be expressed in our Primary Control and throughout our body. If our head is in balance we feel light, easy, confident and generally less stressed. It is interesting that the primary balancing systems, that is, the vestibular and ocular systems are in the head.

Some Alexander teachers refer to the Primary Control as the head–neck–back relationship. Other parts of the body can affect this primary balance, for example, if there is tension in the tongue, the jaw or the eyes, there is a loss of freedom in the balance of the head. If you are tightening your feet, it will limit the freedom in your head–neck–back relationship; if you are releasing your feet onto the floor it will help you free your Primary Control.

When Alexander found a way to avoid the displacement and tightening of his head on the top of his spine, he had discovered a key to resolving his problems. He observed he had a pattern of pulling his head back and down in relation to the spine, which put pressure on his larynx and made him gasp for air. He made a brilliant connection when he noticed this. He was noticing the 'startle pattern' (we all go into 'startle' if we get a shock). At first he thought he only had this 'version of the startle pattern' in performance but on closer observation he realized that he had a milder version of it all the time.

Startle pattern (fight or flight response)

If there is a very loud noise near us that we are not expecting (and sometimes even when we are expecting it), we automatically respond with the startle pattern. Frank Pierce Jones describes the pattern as *remarkably regular*; he goes on – 'It begins with an eye-blink; the head is then thrust forward; the shoulders are raised and the arms stiffened; abdominal muscles shorten; breathing stops and the knees are flexed. The pattern permits minor variations but its primary features are the same.'[2]

Jones studied the 'startle pattern', writing a paper on the subject.[3] His observations backed up Alexander's theories.

Three types of startle pattern

> Because the startle pattern is brief and unexpected it is difficult to observe and more difficult to control. Its chief interest here lies in the fact that it is a model of other slower response patterns.[4]

1 Classic startle pattern

If we are surprised by a very loud noise we go into a sequence of reflex responses. This is called the 'startle pattern'. We blink, suck in air and hold the breath, raise our shoulders as we push the head forward and down in space as we pull the head back in relation to the spine, tighten the abdominal muscles and flex the knees. Chemicals are released in the body that speed up our heart rate and make our restarted breathing faster and shallower. In this condition we are temporarily stronger and hyperalert. That is good news if we have to escape from a burning building but bad news if we have to play a concert.

2 Slow onset startle pattern

When we anticipate a concert with fear of what might go wrong, we develop performance anxiety. The symptoms of performance anxiety are virtually identical to the startle pattern but they usually come on more gradually. We become too fired up with adrenalin over a period of time; the symptoms make accurate, flexible playing just about impossible. However, if we manage to notice the pattern starting, we can avoid the full development of the pattern, and

---

[2]F. P. Jones, *A Technique for Musicians*, Sheldrake Press, London, 1968, p. 9.
[3]F. P. Jones, John Hanson and Florence Gray, 'Startle as a Paradigm of Malposture', *Perceptual and Motor Skills*, 19 (1964), pp. 21–2.
[4]F. P. Jones, *Organisation of Awareness*, Sheldrake Press, London, 1967.

even reverse it, by addressing the Primary Control with Inhibition and Direction.

3 Chronic startle pattern

If we feel under pressure continuously we can develop a state of continuous startle pattern. It makes us appear to lack self-confidence. The head is often held forward in space and the back of the neck tightened. The breathing is restricted and tension is carried throughout the mind and body that restricts free movement and coordination. It is possible to start to reverse this pattern by using Inhibition and Direction.

> Fear, anxiety, fatigue and pain all show postural changes from the norm, which are similar to those seen in startle. In all of them there is a shortening of neck muscles that displaces the head, and which is usually followed by some kind of flexion response, so that the body is drawn into a slightly smaller space.[5]

- You can reverse the onset of startle pattern with inhibition.
- Startle pattern involves a disturbance of the Primary Control.
- If you address the Primary Control you can let go of the startle pattern.

Indirect work

Pedro de Alcantara called his excellent book for musicians, *Indirect Procedures*,[6] an ideal title because it describes the nature of all Alexander work. The conscious, thinking brain on its own makes a very poor job of coordination; the subconscious brain and sensory nervous systems organize it far better. Alexander work is, however, thinking work but the work is always indirect. We are not trying hard to be aware! For example, when we consider the

---

[5]Jones, *Organisation of Awareness*, 1967.
[6]Pedro de Alcantara, *Indirect Procedures*, Clarendon Press, Oxford, 1997.

Primary Control we are intending to facilitate the reflex, automatic rebalancing of the head on the top of the spine – not organize it directly by trying to find the right position and we will not get very far if we 'try hard to be free'.

What are we looking for?

The ideal condition of the Primary Control is one where the head is continuously rebalancing – this is a reflex response. This condition is more likely to exist in us if we are feeling calm, confident and happy. Many times a second the head is rebalanced unless we stop the process by creating residual tension that fixes the relationship. We are not designed to be static or find the correct position and stay there. The name that Alexander chose for this relationship (Primary Control) brings our attention to its importance. It is 'prime' (it is of prime importance to all musicians whether they realize it or not); it is the first relationship to respond to a stimulus; it is the first element we need to think about when considering our Use. 'Control', in this context, is the way the head is continuously reorganized on top of the spine, facilitating other accurate responses throughout the body. The control we are looking for comes from easy and fluid movement; we are allowing something to happen not making it happen. Some people describe this fine balance of the head as 'inner movement'.

Good Primary Control is a prerequisite of functioning well in all activities. It becomes more important when the activity requires fine motor control and good coordination. Being a musician requires coordination of exceptional refinement. If we manage to improve the Primary Control, our playing will become better without any extra practice!

Posture with an open mind

Alexander noticed that we all tend to live life referring to our previous experiences. If we have been told, when young and impressionable, to think about our 'posture' and to try to improve it by sitting or standing up straight, those will be our terms of reference.

Alexander work is a different way of looking at 'posture', we include movement and balance and the idea of full easy stature. We can also include our emotional state as part of our posture. The balanced, full and confident quality that we are looking for can be the indirect result of applying Alexander's 'principles'. The idea of getting the head on the top of the body in the right **position** is a common misunderstanding and an example of what Alexander called, End-gaining (trying hard to get it right). We are actually looking for reflex rebalancing of the head on the spine.

- The Primary Control influences the balance of the whole body.
- The alignment of the whole body influences the Primary Control.
- If we are calm and confident our Primary Control tends to be free.
- If the Primary Control is free we tend to be calm and confident.

Forward and up

The head of a human is designed to release *forward* and *up*, in relation to the spine. If the reflex systems are working well, that will be happening. We can lose that natural tendency if the going gets tough. The most common pattern is for the head to be pushed forward and down in space (see figure p. 35) and the head to be pulled back in relation to the spine to get the face perpendicular. This happens when a wind player takes their head down to their instrument rather than their instrument up to their head.

To re-establish the Forward and Up, we start by noticing the muscular tension that is fixing the head on the top of the spine. We have muscles that fine tune the balance of the head on the spine; these are called the sub-occipital muscles. We intend to stop overtightening these subtle muscles that control the head (Inhibition). That unfixes the head and improves balancing. You can think of the top of your spine, that is, the top of your neck, moving back and up in space as your head releases forward in relation to the spine (Direction) – this encourages your spine to lengthen.

Primary Control

- Allow your neck to be free
- So that your head goes Forward and Up
- In such a way that your back lengthens and widens
- Soften the back of your neck
- Think the top of your spine back and up

Use semi-supine

It is possible to get a very good sense of releasing the head/neck muscles by lying down in semi-supine. There is a photo on page 131 that shows the position. You lie on your back on the floor with your legs folded so your knees are going up. You put a suitable book or books under your head. The books under your head need to be a certain height so your head is aligned with your spine; this way your spine will be free to lengthen and your back free to widen. You give your head and neck over to the full effect of gravity – you may well feel the release that is possible. As you lay there you can appreciate the lack of need for muscular tension in the neck, the books under your head do the work. When you leave the floor and stand up you will sense your head is freer to balance. Chapter 13 looks at semi-supine in detail.

Don't pull your head towards your instrument

If we Inhibit pulling our head towards the instrument, we are trying to leave the Primary Control to be governed by the reflex system. This encourages the extensor muscles to lengthen the spine.

If we contradict the habit of pulling the head towards the instrument, by thinking the head 'up', we are again encouraging the organization of the head and spine by the in-built anti-gravity reflex. This weakens the habit of pulling the head down.

- We are designed so the head tips forward and goes up.
- Don't pull your head towards the instrument.
- Think your head Forward and Up.
- Avoid fixing your head on the spine.

You and your instrument

Taichi demonstrating easy balance with his violin - the set up should always facilitate the Primary Control.

You should not look for a position that is fixed in relation to your instrument. It is good to have a dynamic relationship that allows the head to be free to rebalance while you are playing. There are various devices that help musicians support their instrument, for example, harnesses for some wind instruments or a stand on which to rest your tuba.

Crissman Taylor (a violin playing Alexander teacher) is creating wonderful set-ups for fiddle players of all shapes and sizes. You can see her work at www.violinistinbalance.nl/

Allow your head to rebalance

The last sentence is worth repeating for all musicians; *the set-up should always facilitate the Primary Control.* If you are a wind or brass player there are various technical issues relating to the embouchure and the instrument; the trick is to include freedom in the Primary Control when achieving those. Getting the air moving out of your body and through the instrument will be more in your control with a rebalancing head. Alexander's breathing improved when he sorted out his Primary Control. All instruments have their challenges, for example, many cellists create a problem for themselves by accommodating the C peg by displacing their head. (For some useful ideas, see Chapter 20: Instrumental technique). Alexander's balance and coordination improved when he unfixed his Primary Control.

Build your relationship with your instrument, starting with Primary Control

The Primary Control is the best place to start building the new approach to any activity. If you are having a fresh look at an activity, inhibit the old response in the Primary Control and you have a new pathway that can lead to better overall pattern.

Assuming you pull your head down to your instrument; if you do manage to inhibit the old pattern and release your head Forward and Up, into a new sense of balance, it might not feel like 'you' playing the instrument! If you change what you are doing you will not feel the same. Alexander noticed that this is the experience for everyone. You may feel like you are not trying to play well or you might feel separate from your instrument (for a while); yet, this could well be the path towards far better results. This work helps us to understand the nature of change. As we change we feel different for a time until we get used to the new pattern. It is ideal if a reliable friend or colleague is hearing the results because they may well have a better chance of assessing the potential of this new pattern. They do not have to cope with the unfamiliar feelings that you are dealing with. If you are practising alone, you might choose to record your practice to assess the effect of any changes without the new feelings influencing your perceptions. It is, of course, useful to video-record this work, but consider carefully what you are hearing when you are watching the video. Music is primarily heard rather than seen.

Free the jaw

The mouth is closed by right tension in the muscles attached to the jaw. We normally have our mouth closed. As with all activities, it is good to have the necessary tension but no more. We tend to restrict our breathing when we clamp the mouth shut. The freedom at the atlanto-occipital joint tends to be lost if you overtighten the jaw. If you are gritting your teeth, or pressing your tongue to the roof of your mouth, during a 'difficult bit', part of the difficulty will be because you have lost freedom at the top of your spine. The jaw articulates with the skull, just in front of the ear, very near the top of the spine. The muscles that organize the jaw have an influence on head-balancing muscles. If you think of gravity affecting your jaw, it helps you release extra tension.

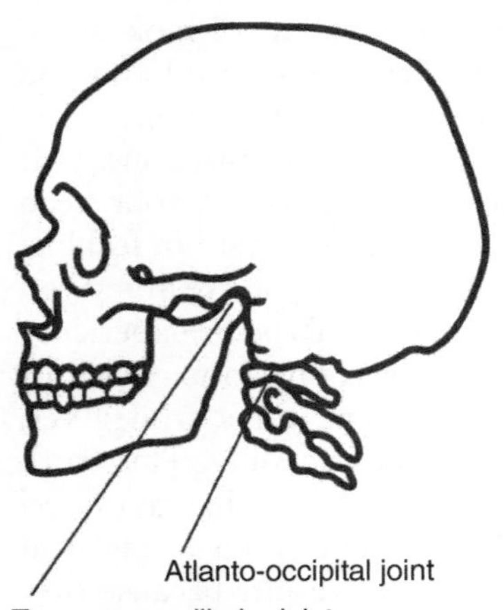

- Soften your face to release your jaw
- Soften your tongue
- Find where your jaw joins onto your skull

Free the jaw

Experiment with less tension

If your jaw is involved with playing your instrument bring your attention to how much tension is required; if you are a singer your jaw is obviously very important; experiment with doing less; keep reducing tension until it doesn't work well; you have now found the minimum tension; revisit it to check up from time to time. If you do not need to use your jaw when playing your instrument, notice that although your lips may well be lightly together, you can leave your teeth slightly apart.

- You don't need to hold your teeth together.

Can you speak?

Many of us tighten the throat when playing. If you play an instrument where it is reasonable to speak while playing, for example, keyboard instruments, percussion, cello, see if you can! You may find that you are caught up in your vocal mechanism. Practise speaking and playing at the same time – you may have to work at this for a while. The tension in your vocal system will be getting in the way of your breathing and Primary Control. You could try reading a newspaper on your music stand out aloud, while playing something from memory. If you are a wind/brass player, imagine speaking while you play, you will sense unnecessary tension if it is there. In fact, you may be asked to speak into your instrument, by some contemporary composers, for special effects, so this is good practise for such a piece. Your sound will change when you release vocal tension but there will be other benefits that you may feel as freedom and improved coordination. If you are a singer, you will have worked on this already but you may well be creating unnecessary tension in the area of your jaw. If it is difficult to let go of your jaw tension, you may find Alexander's procedure, the Whispered 'Ah' very helpful (see p. 101).

- Look after your Primary Control when you are organizing your relationship with your instrument.
- Free your vocal mechanism when you are playing.

Evolution

Our upright anatomy has evolved over millions of years. If we pull our head down we wind the evolutionary clock back. We have become upright to gain a greater range of flexible movements and to free the arms for sophisticated activities, like playing musical instruments! The head is at the top of the body making it easy to see the world around us.

When babies first learn to sit up, they have their head balancing perfectly. Babies have not had a chance to develop the extra muscle power to hold the head anywhere other than in balance. When we learn to stand and walk, balancing is still the name of the game. If you watch a toddler, you can see the head leading and the body following. Some people never lose the free balancing of the head. Most of us need to re-establish the freedom after we lose it.

When we engage with something that interests us, the Primary Control is part of our connection with it. You can see if someone is interested in what you are saying, when you look at their head–neck–back relationship. It is important to notice how our Primary Control changes as we engage with our instrument. Our attitude to anything is expressed through our whole body but the first response will always be in the Primary Control. Confident people usually have a good head–neck–back relationship.

Heroes

As musicians we probably have a collection of players that we admire above all others. The brilliant players of all instruments have brilliant Primary Control. If you want to play as well as a musical hero, start by emulating their Primary Control. It is worth looking on YouTube at a few of the all time greats: Heifetz, Pavarotti, Rubenstein, and others.

So, the Primary Control has a profound effect on your coordination. It should be an absolute priority whatever your instrument. If you think there is a contradiction between the received wisdom on how to play your instrument and your understanding of free Primary Control, keep an open mind about it.

Summary

- Good Primary Control is fundamental to good coordination.
- Consider your Primary Control first.
- The Primary Control can be reflex-facilitated.
- The Primary Control influences the rest of the body.
- We are not looking for a position for the head.
- We are designed for the head to go Forward and Up.
- Your attitude affects your Primary Control.
- Consider the Primary Control in your relationship with your instrument.
- Free your voice for better Primary Control.

Student quotes

I find myself comparing the organisation of my head, neck and back to that of a dolmen. The Irish countryside is dotted with these megalithic structures that may look to the casual observer like random slabs of stone, but they are perfectly arranged. My head, neck and back are also cleverly designed, and sometimes I forget this, leading to tension and later, discomfort. When I compare the structure of my spine and head to that of the dolmens, I am reminded of the importance of my Primary Control. If one of the stones of a dolmen is misaligned, the structure will fall, sooner or later.

Mary Kelly, viola player

Today, I became aware for the first time that when I play, I tilt my head quite far backwards. I have learnt now that this can only hinder my playing by causing the muscles in my neck to contract. This essentially is unnecessary tension. Tension in this area can be very restricting, especially as these muscles are positioned around my spinal cord.

Charlie Buchanan, trumpeter

CHAPTER SIX

Inhibition

The immediate result of Alexandrian inhibition is a sense of freedom as if a heavy garment that has been hampering all of your movements has been removed.

F. P. Jones[1]

Inhibition is often seen as thoughtful poise in activity

[1]Jones, *Organisation of Awareness*, 1967.

Inhibition is the key to change. Alexander used the word, Inhibition to name the process of precluding a habit so you can choose what you are doing. At any moment you can stop, to choose what you are going to do next.

- At any moment you can stop to choose.

Sigmund Freud used the word 'inhibition' too and maybe we are more familiar with Freud's use of the word with its aura of emotional suppression. Alexander used the word with the scientific meaning – an inhibitor in a chemical reaction slows down or stops the reaction, the application of Alexander's conception of Inhibition slows down or stops your reaction to something. When we use the word Inhibition it is about choices. It is good to recognize that you can choose to stop your activity at any time to think about how you are doing it, especially when you are practising. Then you can have another go and handle it differently.

When Alexander was practising recitation in front of the mirror; he would stop and start again when he noticed his habit had slipped back into the way he was reciting. If we want to make changes as quickly as possible, that is what we need to do.

- Inhibition is used before the habit is repeated.

The displacement of the head

When Alexander stopped pulling his head back and down, that was an example of inhibition. What was left, as the new status quo, was his body's reflex response to gravity – his head was going Forward and Up. Alexander famously said, 'Stop doing the wrong thing and the right thing does itself.'

He found he had to stop to give himself a chance to consider what he was doing with his head. If he did not stop but simply decided to do something different and then recited, he could see in the mirror that his habit took over and the change either did not happen or was short lived. He found it useful to think, 'Stop!' or 'No!' to get consciously into that moment before the habit happened. This stopping idea is not a freezing and should be in no way static. The 'No!' is, unusually, not a negative because it brings about a positive habit-free response.

- Give yourself permission to stop.
- Choose to tune in.

Glen Park makes it clear that this special moment is a particular state of being: 'Inhibiting a reaction to a stimulus means simply not responding, neither reacting nor resisting reaction which is also a form of reaction.'[2]

> James Allsopp (saxophonist) talking to students at LCATT Alexander training course, 2010:
>
> Inhibition is an absence of interference that allows the right thing to do itself.
>
> Inhibition is being receptive, without an agenda; receptive to messages both internal and external without seeking to control our response to these messages.

Alexander realized that three significant options or choices were available at the moment of Inhibition.

1. To do what he would have done habitually: It is very good that he wrote this because we can see clearly the intention is free will or conscious choice.
2. To do nothing, or avoid the activity: It is very good to choose this response sometimes, because it acknowledges the importance of avoiding the negative pattern. If you are prepared to not play your musical instrument, because you want to change what you do, you have acknowledged the importance of the change. Your emotional commitment to playing your instrument is being challenged by your emotional commitment to look after yourself.
3. To do something differently: This is the most frequently taken choice. For example, having noticed when you sing

---

[2]Glen Park, *The Art of Changing*, Ashgrove Press, Bath, 1989, p. 104.

that you tighten your neck, pulling the head into the spine – you then choose to direct the head Forward and Up to leave the Primary Control in your non-singing mode allowing you to sing with a free rebalancing head on the spine.

Applying inhibition

Let us say that you are about to start singing or playing. You know that the plan is to sing or play but you avoid just doing it by pausing to think about how you will do it this time. So, the conscious mind is stepping in to avoid the subconscious way of doing it. You are now in a new situation; you have elevated your awareness of your habit, or your *set*, and are now in Conscious Control of the situation.

> A **'set'** in this sense of the term is an attitude of expectancy, which facilitates a learned response. You are most apt to become aware of a 'set' when the expected does not occur as when a shovel full of snow is heavier than it looks, or there is one less stair to climb than you anticipated.[3]

At this time you can consider your three options described in the previous paragraph. If you choose option 3 you can give yourself some Directions and stay in Conscious Control as you go ahead with playing or singing.

If you are going to improve your instrumental technique or performance in any way, it is usually necessary to stop doing the old thing before you can get something new working for you. For example: If a musician thoroughly learns a piece of music but learns a wrong note and then has it brought to their notice by a colleague or teacher, it is necessary to stop playing the wrong note and start playing the correct one. That is not always easy. I expect most musicians have planned to correct a note, made a mark in the score to remind themselves to make the change *and then played the wrong note again*! There is also the experience of the critical note arriving in the performance and having the experience that your

---

[3]Jones, *Freedom to Change*, 2003.

head is telling you to play the correct note but your body is trying to play the wrong note and an unsatisfactory compromise is the result. In that scenario we have not completely stopped (inhibited) playing the wrong note.

- When the old pattern is really inhibited, the change has been learnt.

We will now consider applying inhibition to specific muscular tension:

For example: If you push your left shoulder up to hold your violin you would be better of changing the pattern. If you decided to hold your shoulder down you would probably end up with increased tension and discomfort. The habit would be pushing the shoulder up and your willpower would be pulling the shoulder down, overpowering the muscles pushing up. You might look good for your publicity photo but you will not have the free movement of the shoulder, arm and hand that is good for playing. This is where inhibition comes in!

- Inhibition is sometimes all you need to make a complete change.

Referring back to Alexander's three choices:

1 You remember that you have the 'shoulder pushing up habit' but you decide this time you will not change anything, that is, choose to play in the usual manner.
2 You remember that you have the 'shoulder pushing up habit' and consider whether, this time, you will not play the instrument so as to avoid this negative habit.
3 You intend to avoid pushing your shoulder up – it becomes your priority. You Direct your head up and your shoulders away from each other – maintaining those Directions, notice the effect of gravity on your shoulder and notice how you play.
   - You don't have to get anything right; you just have to remember you have choices.

It is important that you make the *change* the priority and not the musical result, at least for the moment. If initially you find you don't play so well, stay interested and committed to the change. If you are 'inhibiting' a habit, *that* is your priority and the present end in mind! When you have fully inhibited the negative use of the shoulder your technique will have improved and the new technique will be available in future. Your playing, when you have improved your Use, will be more coordinated and flexible. Often such a change improves your playing immediately, in which case it is easier to stay with the process of change.

> Relating these ideas to practice the most efficient way of solving a technical obstacle is not only to identify the problem but also to find a conscious state where there is a moment of true choice before executing an action that counterbalances the problem. By being aware of directing a personal thought, an action of any size can be performed that contradicts habit. The possibility of change is then opened up to allow your practising to grow or develop relating to its tone speed and accuracy etc.
>
> Cassie Yukawa, pianist

Start small with inhibition

So you can see how important Inhibition is in this learning process. See if you can enjoy playing with these ideas. You could initially practise putting inhibition into your life with small, easy to challenge habits. Maybe start brushing your teeth from a different corner of your mouth each morning. Put your watch on the other wrist or open doors with the other hand. Walk a different route to the station.

- Inhibition helps us to avoid being a slave to our habits.

Inhibition and getting out of a chair

In Alexander lessons, teachers often look at the stimulus of getting in and out of a chair (a frequent daily activity) without tightening the neck. The skill of applying inhibition is transferable to other activities. When you are getting the hang of these less emotive everyday activities, you can move on to bigger challenges. We have a lot of emotional investment in playing our musical instrument; that makes applying inhibition and changing a bigger issue.

- Start using inhibition on less emotive activities.
- Notice if you rush your everyday activities.
- Inhibition becomes a transferable skill.
- Move onto working on your playing.

Stay tuned into your kinaesthetic sense

We can tune into our kinaesthetic sense (sense of movement) to monitor how our changes are going. When Alexander started work on inhibiting his pattern, he found it reasonably easy making the change when just starting to recite. Once he got involved with the text he had a tendency to go back to his habit. He found he needed to make the awareness a constant, like a musician does with intonation, tempo, and so on. In this state of continuous awareness, change was possible and the new pattern could be learnt. Inhibition is part of your toolkit for change, both psychophysically and musically.

Inhibition – a flexible state of being

Another way of seeing inhibition is as a *state* of not reacting automatically in any situation. It should, however, look normal and not fixed or static. If your 'not reacting' takes a noticeable amount of time, you will appear disengaged from the situation. Good Use looks flowing and natural. When first working on Inhibition you might take a little more time to respond but this should soon become less and less time to the point where you are simply aware, and the response does not require any extra time. If you display an apparent thoughtful awareness, because you are avoiding immediate thoughtless responses, it is usually seen as wisdom or self-possession, on stage it looks calm and confident.

Presence and creativity through Inhibition

If our habit is to think about the past, for example, 'I played better in the rehearsal' or the future, for example, 'here comes that difficult bit', we can apply Inhibition and so leave ourselves more truly in the present. If you are a composer or you are a player involved in creative improvisation you can use Inhibition to avoid predictable responses. Awareness that you can be making continuous choices on every level puts you in a creative driving seat.

- In performance spontaneity is available if automatic playing is 'inhibited'.
- Inhibition becomes easy – you are present and ready for action.

A final reassurance

We feel connected with our instrument because of the familiar sensations that return when we play as we have in the past. When we inhibit something in our playing with a view to change, we can get a sense of disconnection or insecurity. This will evaporate when the change is learnt. The new, 'improved' pattern will feel just as connected and secure as the old pattern when it is the new status quo.

Summary

- Inhibit any unnecessary tension in the primary control first.
- Identify the habit.
- Notice your habit or 'set'.
- Experiment with the process and make it fun.
- Remember you are choosing to change the habit.
- Stop doing the wrong thing and the right thing does itself.
- Let go of the desire to achieve the result.

- Inhibition comes before the habit.
- There are at least three choices available.
- Inhibition involves heightened awareness.
- Change feels unfamiliar at first.
- As you develop the skill of inhibition it takes less and less time.
- Inhibition helps bring you into the present.
- You can apply inhibition to all types of human response.
- If you inhibit default behaviour you become more spontaneous.
- When you have completely inhibited the old pattern you will feel as secure and connected with your instrument as you did before the change.

Student quotes

You should never try to change or enhance breathing directly. You inhibit the extra effort or gestures you are making, like pulling your head back to open your mouth. In its simplest form, breathing is not something you do, instead it is something that happens to you when you don't get in the way. That is what's left in place when you inhibit the unnecessary effort.

Suzannah Watson, flautist

This inhibition can be applied when performing a piece of music. Instead of playing in a way that has developed through repetitive practice, we can make the choice to feel and listen to the space between the notes and obtain a freedom to respond in a way that aids the flow of phrases instead of impeding them. We can choose to be aware of certain technical aspects that are necessary, whilst all the time considering the ultimate goal, of phrasing and shaping the structure of the entire piece.

Kate Robinson, violinist

CHAPTER SEVEN

Direction

There is no such thing as a right position, but there is such a thing as a right direction.[1]

F. M. Alexander

With Direction we can look energised and capable of anything

---

[1]F. M. Alexander, *Articles and Lectures*, Mouritz, London, 1995.

So, what we are looking for, when we consider Direction?

Good Use is often what you see in young children when they are happily playing. They are not thinking about their Use but they are displaying good Use. We can restore good Use by using Direction to re-establish expansion and ease. When an Alexander student restores good Use they often say they feel light in movement and find greater pleasure in practice and performance. Direction is thinking but it might not be thinking as you have understood it before – it includes the body, the sensory nervous system in particular; it is thinking by the whole person.

Direction is one of the cornerstones of Alexander's Technique. Direction is part of your toolkit for change, taking you towards Alexander's idea of Conscious Control.

When you see a healthy tree stretching into the sky, moving gently in the breeze, you see natural direction. The most beautiful dancers, some athletes, martial artists and great musicians display this graceful coordinated quality. We are all capable of it, either now or in the future. Direction is described in Eastern traditions as chi or energy.

Alexander's idea of Direction is a thought or intention, a willing or wishing that allows a flow of energy or subtle movement. Direction contradicts the negative tendencies of too much tension or overrelaxation and helps develop a more reliable sensory awareness; it is chosen constructive thought.

As an example: If someone's habit is to push their shoulders up when they bring their clarinet up for playing, with Direction they can change it. They might use the Direction, 'allow the shoulders to release away from each other', as they prepare to play their instrument.

Direction can also be a simple confirmation of a good tendency, for example, 'think the head up and release the sitting bones down onto the chair'; those Directions freshen up the anti-gravity reflex responses that are built into all of us, allowing us to sit in easy upright balance.

Direction is not about forcing anything or making something happen directly – that would be an idea like 'holding the shoulders down' or sitting up straight. Note that we are not thinking of simply 'putting our posture right'. The idea is – to use your *thought* or your *intention* or your *will* or *wish* to contradict the unhelpful habit.

- Conscious Direction is thinking.
- Direction is effortless.
- Direction is part of your toolkit for change.

Seeing Direction in this 'Non-doing' light makes it a perfect companion to Inhibition. These ideas encourage a re-establishment of the free flowing, coordinated movement that came naturally to us when we were young. This is why Alexander described his work as 're-education'.

Non-doing

Non-doing is when you are not aiming to get results directly or by trying too hard. You are not doing nothing! You are getting interested in letting go of unnecessary tension and effort – this allows the reflex responses that make movement as coordinated and easy as possible. The experience of movement then becomes light, free and connected. These sensations are often experienced, at first, in an Alexander lesson with a teacher, with hands on. The teacher will facilitate a connected easy movement from the student. The student allows something new to take place. After the lesson the student looks into discovering a similar ease, by using their own Directions to take the place of the teacher's influence.

> I now realise why it is the thinking of the Directions and not the doing that is important. Even if you feel or see no difference, a change will be taking place, for the better. When I relate this to my violin playing, I develop much more control over my movements. If I start from thinking the Directions, I am usually still, therefore; when I make even the smallest movement to pick up the violin, I notice my response to stimuli much more sensitively than if didn't stop and think.
>
> Anna Cashell, violinist

So you could see Direction as tapping into healthy responses. Indeed, it is often possible to see healthy, free and perfectly coordinated Use in people who have never heard of F. M. Alexander. Unfortunately it is true to say – that does not seem to be the norm for musicians! Perhaps it's the tyranny of 'getting it right' that seems to prevail in the classical music world. Miles Davis said, 'Don't worry about wrong notes, there aren't any.'

Playing musical instruments can be comfortable

It is possible to play all musical instruments in complete comfort, if our Use is well balanced and flexible. The instruments have developed and been redesigned for our convenience. There are modifications that make it possible for almost any human to play any musical instrument. Playing any instrument comfortably is possible when you see that it is the way you use yourself in relation to the instrument that makes the difference.

Discomfort is distracting and it is usually caused by unnecessary tension or overrelaxation. Overrelaxation makes you feel heavy and less moveable. Tension reduces sensation, so if you have extra tension you will be missing out on sensory feedback that could help your playing.

- Direction is a big part of combating discomfort.

The best time to work out how to hold, stand or sit comfortably with your instrument is when you start learning it. Of course, it is never too late to sort it out. You are looking for balance and freedom to move. It is always worth revisiting these fundamentals to check that you are still well balanced with your instrument. A moment or two when you start practising is time well spent. That way you can expect to enjoy playing and stay comfortable for the whole of your playing life.

- You can be comfortable when you play your instrument.
- Balance and freedom with the instrument can be re-established using Direction.

Different approaches to Direction

Words

There are several ways of 'directing' that are in common use. Alexander used words. He thought, 'let the neck be free so the head goes Forward and Up'. He chose those words because he had analysed his pattern of Use and realized he tended to pull his head back and down, in relation to the spine – 'head Forward and Up' was a counteraction of his negative habit. He gave the same Directions to his students if they had the same pattern as him.

On further consideration of his Use he realized that he had a tendency to shorten and narrow his back, so Alexander added 'in such a way that the back lengthens and widens'. Your comfort, coordination and confidence improve if your back is lengthening and widening.

Classic Alexander Directions include:

- Allow the neck to be free.
- To let the head go Forward and Up.
- In such a way that the back lengthens and widens.
- Send the shoulders away from each other.
- Send the knees forward and away.
- Sense your feet on the floor.

Directing using images

Alexander's acolytes, on the early training courses, discussed all aspects of the work including Direction and some of them came up with other approaches to it, such as using images. So you might direct by thinking of your head floating up like a balloon or imagining your head being like a ball bobbling about on the top of a fountain of water. Some people think their 'head up like a rocket' when they get out of a chair. The use of images seems to work better than words for some people. Alexander was an actor; he loved the written and spoken word; he was a 'words person'.

We were both initially taught using words as Directions. Over the years we visited different teachers and every one of them taught Direction in a slightly different, personal way, just like instrumental or singing teachers teaching technique. We are very glad to have used both ideas, both are successful. As teachers of the Alexander Technique we realize that some students are more inspired by one way of working than the other.

Another approach

As in many walks of life, there is third way in Alexander, not to mention the fourth and subsequent ways. Marjory Barstow, who was one of the first Alexander trainees to receive Alexander's blessing to teach the Technique, encouraged her students to take personal responsibility to move the head up (or counteract whatever habit they were working on), but to do it *delicately*. 'Marj' kept reminding her students to do it *delicately*.[2] The effect is the same as using words and images. You can develop a sense of the level of delicacy in movement by experimentation with an open mind. Marj encouraged an approach that included conscious movement. We are designed to move and that is what happens when we 'direct', it is very delicate movement (this is very different from effortful pulling or pushing). We create more freedom at the joints and movement becomes more fluent, accurate and beautiful.

Movement with a directed quality

It is effective to direct your attention to the quality of your movements. You can use your imagination to add freedom, buoyancy, poise and lightness to any gesture or activity. If you are looking for ease in the balance with your instrument, the qualities you choose to include in your direction can help avoid heaviness, effort, tightness, and so on.

If we give an RCM student many lessons we introduce them to different ways of 'directing' and help them find the best way for them. We experiment with them and are very happy to have

---

[2]We heard her teaching and using the expression.

all these possible approaches. This is like versatile instrumental technique – several different ways of practising.

Working with vision

There are more ways, of course, of working on Direction. We feel it is appropriate to mention the work of teachers who work with the sense of vision. They encourage an awareness of the quality of your vision. We usually enjoy whatever we are doing when we are seeing effortlessly. It makes a big difference to reading and understanding, if you are in good lighting conditions. Well-lit concert platforms make reading music easy and a pleasure. It is difficult not to pull your head towards the music and tighten your eyes when the lighting is poor – both of those gestures unbalance your Primary Control and do not improve your eyesight! Your Primary Control tends to be free and balanced when you are seeing effortlessly.

- Allow your vision to move lightly on the music.

A brief experiment with visual Direction

As you are reading this, notice how focused you are on the words that you are reading. Notice how much of the environment you can see while you are reading. Notice the colour that is around you and where the light is stronger and weaker. Allow yourself to see the grey of the page behind these words. Look away from the book, into the distance, and then back to the book with the suggested thoughts in mind. Notice how you are feeling. Many people feel refreshed; it is more comfortable to read and they are more alert. If you feel a change when you try this, you have directed your attention through the visual system to make that change.

Spatial Direction and awareness

Some teachers use Direction in conjunction with 'spatial awareness'. This is a very powerful way to create a sense presence in the environment (e.g. the concert hall) as well as Direction in the body.

Try experimenting with these Directions:

- Imagine the space between your shoulders and between you and the walls either side of you.
- When sitting, imagine the space between your head and your sitting bones, the floor beneath you and the ceiling above you.
- Imagine the space between the front and the back of your body and the walls in front and behind you.

We feel different in a room with a high ceiling compared with a low ceiling. If we include an awareness of our environment our Direction has more meaning and will be more integrated with our whole system. It is deep practice to bring attention to our body and not lose the world around us. That is the ideal state in which to play a musical instrument.

Opposition in Direction

When we direct we can benefit from using opposing Directions at the same time. It is the way we are designed to work. The head moves away from the feet, as the feet move away from the head. The hands move away from the back, as the back moves away from the hands. The shoulders move away from each other. Putting in place these opposing Directions encourages the body to expand rather than contract. They are also more connected with the whole body than single Directions. We see this in nature, for example, the top of the tree grows up as the roots grow down.

- There are many ways of directing
- You can direct your attention
- Use opposing Directions
- Stay in touch with the environment
- Direct in relation to the whole body

Direct your Primary Control first

All the different ways of directing are looking for improved Use. The first area to include in your Directional thoughts is always the Primary Control because all movements are initiated there, whether you are applying the Alexander principles or not. Good Primary Control is like having your instrument in tune before playing it. Direction tunes you, ready for action.

To recap: Direct the head in relation to the spine first. Imagine your head releasing Forward and Up into balance on top of your spine and moving in the direction your spine is pointing, thus encouraging the back to lengthen and widen. If you find your head is forward and down in space, direct the top of your spine back and up as you release the head into balance. When this all happens we are well on the way to a whole-body coordination. This releasing Forward and Up of the head into free easy balance is part of your instrumental technique.

Build up Directions with your instrument

If you play the oboe, for instance, you may well tip your head to set up a good relationship with the reed. This gesture is applicable to many instruments. It is important that you do not pull your head down onto your instrument. So to be clear: Apply a moment of Inhibition; you don't intend to 'do it as usual'. Think of your 'Primary Directions' – releasing the sub-occipital muscles. This gets the head tipping forward in relation to the spine; now think of the head going up in the direction the spine is pointing. Then you are ready to add secondary Directions, for example, imagine your shoulders moving away from each other or away from your head as your hands lead your arms towards the playing 'set-up' for your instrument. The intention is to have your head freely balancing while you play your instrument.

This thinking may take a little extra practice time to put in place *at first*, but when it becomes familiar it will take no extra time. The initial extra time is well worth spending. Your Direction will be part of the quality of movement and your movement *is you playing your instrument.*

If this is all working easily for you, you can add 'more Directions'; you might think of your elbows moving away from your shoulders and the wrists away from the elbows. Think of your ribs moving up and down, like bucket handles, in relation to the spine and sternum. If you are enjoying adding Directions, there is almost no limit but even if you just choose to work on your Primary Control you will be gaining real, tangible benefit. With reduced tension from good Direction you cope with the vagaries of your instrument more easily and you find interacting musically with other players an easy pleasure.

Your Alexander teacher can guide the development of new Directions but you will find it interesting to experiment with them yourself. The new Directions are added like new elements to your instrumental technique. They may require some well-considered attention at first but when they become part of how you play your instrument they are available whenever you think about them. It is like learning sections of a new piece and putting them together.

- Design Directions that enhance your instrumental technique.
- Direct your Primary Control first.
- Experiment with your Directions.

Create sequences and 'key Directions'

For example: If you are an organist and you are aiming to work on pedalling, think your head up as you find your sitting bones on the bench; connect with your lengthening and widening back; think of the knees moving forward and away from the hip joints as you change notes; send the ankles away from your knees; send your heels and toes away from your ankles. Notice the resistance from the pedals through your feet and through your legs into your upper body.

Use key Directions for performance

Detailed Directional thinking needs to be simplified for performance. When you have built up a sequence of Directions, you can often access the whole sequence by creating key Directions, for example, think of sending your head up and your feet towards the pedals. If you have set this up, the whole sequence can spring into action by thinking the key Directions. The result will be effortless, enjoyable playing.

- Build your sequences of Directions in practice time.
- Create and practise key Directions.
- The result will be effortless, enjoyable playing.

Direct in the context of the whole body

The Primary Control has the effect of a key Direction; it helps to reorganize the whole system. It is good to consider your Directions in the context of the whole body and your environment. We have been considering different Directions like pieces of a jigsaw. The pieces of the jigsaw fit together, to make up the big picture that is the well-coordinated Self.

Practice Direction in your daily life

It is good to be practising Direction during everyday activities. Sitting on a chair, you can think of balancing on your sitting bones with your head going up above them. Getting into and out of a chair, you can think of your knees going forward and away from your low back. Direct your attention to the environment and become aware of your balance, breathing and vision. As you work on directing in everyday activities you bring yourself into a flexible unity, making it possible for you to function in a more coordinated way, whatever you are doing, including playing your musical instrument.

- Directions help us to get in touch with ourselves and the environment.

Student quotes

I have found that by integrating the directing of my head upwards and my shoulders outwards, as I am consciously working my way through a musical problem zone, I am far more likely to stay in control.

Cassie Yukawa, pianist

Before my understanding of Use I had been concentrating on the release of tension in my shoulder during playing. This had never worked because as soon as my attention was directed elsewhere, for example, whilst playing a technically demanding passage, the tension returned. However, when I considered the use of my body as a whole and concentrated on the basic Alexander principles of lengthening the spine, and widening the back, directing my shoulders towards my elbows, my elbows towards my wrists and my wrists towards my fingertips, the unnecessary tension was removed and replaced by an efficient use of the body as a whole.

Kate Robinson, violinist

CHAPTER EIGHT

Attention and awareness

The mind is like a parachute, it works best when it is open.

Frank Zappa

Awareness, as I conceive it, is a general, unfocussed condition in which a person is wide awake and alert to whatever may be going on without being concentrated on anything in particular. Attention on the other hand, is focussed on some particular aspect of the field. It has been compared to a spotlight on a dark stage.[1]

F. P. Jones

Presence

Jones goes on to suggest that, with work on it, we can intelligently balance our awareness and attention to bring ourselves into the ideal state for playing music. The 'ideal state', when musicians are going to give something their attention, is 'a spotlight on a well-lit stage'. Then we can remain truly present.

Ulf Tolle (horn player and Alexander teacher),[2] says, 'I have discovered that I waste a lot of energy on stage by desiring to be some place other than where I am, whereas the only possibility is to acknowledge where I am and to be there.'

The voice in your head

Do you experience mental chatter? Are your thoughts constructively involved in your practice or performance? If you do have a voice in your head, you may lose awareness of what's going on around you. If you find there is a voice giving you a commentary, it is tempting to listen to it. It can be an effort to ignore it and that effort can be distracting. If you accept that 'the voice is there', but decide you are not listening to it because you are more interested in other things that are going on; you can redirect your awareness to what you are sensing in the context of the big picture, that is, everything that is going on around you. You are reorganizing your priorities. You can develop external and internal awareness in the appropriate balance, Frank Pierce Jones's ideal state for the musician.

---

[1]Jones, *Organization of Awareness*, 1968.
[2]Ulf Tolle, *Direction Magazine*, vol. 1, no. 8.

- Be where you are – be present.
- Direct your attention away from the voice in your head.
- You can choose the balance of your awareness and attention.

Internal and external awareness

As musicians, we can use awareness of our internal feedback when playing our instrument. We can be sensing our movement and the resistance and vibrations from our instrument. We can have a vibrant sense of how we relate to our instrument and how it is all working. We also use our external awareness of our colleagues and the space we are playing in when playing in an ensemble. The balance between the internal and external awareness is not a constant because the demands of playing any piece of music will be constantly changing.

It can be that a musician is drawn to their internal awareness (because they are determined to play their instrument as well as possible!) to the exclusion of what is going on around them – this usually causes ensemble problems. If you could hear a musician's playing, on its own, you may hear very good playing – but a beautifully played note or phrase in the wrong place is not a good contribution to the performance. In fact we need to have our attention on external matters as a priority because a poorly played note at the right time makes a much better contribution than the beautifully played note at the wrong time! We are, of course, aiming to put both external and internal awareness in place at the same time so we play beautifully and in the right place.

- Balance your internal and external awareness.
- In ensemble playing external awareness is a priority.

Multi-tasking

As musicians we accept that we must multi-task when we perform or practise. No musician would say that they do not include intonation in their continuous awareness, nor would they admit to leaving out an awareness of rhythm, style, articulation, resonance, phrasing, ensemble or balance, to name some of the elements in playing music. As we gain experience and develop as musicians we become more capable of the multi-tasking and so become known as better musicians because those are qualities that are highly valued. Any activity, including playing music, will have essential components that need to be appreciated and organized into an ideal balance as we develop the skill.

> Awareness is knowledge of what is going on while it is happening – of what you are doing while you are doing it. It is a generalized alertness to present events.[3]

If we consider including Alexander work in our playing we can see it as a way of refining our musical skills. It is a way of understanding and raising awareness of what we are doing that makes any activity more absorbing and easier. We become more present with the 'essential components' of being a musician from a psychophysical (mind and body) angle. You could say it is not an extra thing to think about, more an attitude to what you already, as a musician, choose to think about – you become more aware of that choosing.

- Alexander thinking makes playing music more absorbing and easier.

Psychophysical unity

Your mind and body are continuously affecting each other. If you think you have left your phone on the bus that is just leaving the bus stop you will feel the effect throughout your body; again your whole body will tell you when you find it in your pocket, after all. When your body calms down, because it can sense the phone is where it should be, your mind becomes calm and ready for the next challenge in life. If you want to perform spontaneously, expressively or what we might call 'well', being aware of the psychophysical reality will facilitate your performance. How you focus your attention and what you are aware of, will be affecting your physical ability to play your instrument and your ensemble skills. The tension, pressure, relaxation and movement, including your breathing, affect your ability to think clearly and make decisions.

---

[3]Jones, *Organization of Awareness*, 1968.

Patrick Macdonald said: 'Concentration usually raises muscle tension and hinders awareness.'[4]

- Your mind and body continuously affect each other.
- Be aware of your Whole Self.

Spatial awareness

Our overall functioning benefits from good spatial awareness; we can include a sense of the environment that we are in. If we become overly interested in what is in front of us we can lose the sense of the space above our head, behind our back or the ground under our feet. If we direct our attention into the whole environment around us we usually come into balance and find freedom in mind and body. This awareness of the environment is part of the overall awareness that can include our internal, psychophysical awareness of what we are doing. There is not a divide unless we decide there is! As musicians we need internal awareness to maintain good instrumental and performing technique. We need external awareness to interact with our colleagues and the audience. Our spatial awareness also helps us to interact with our instrument when we are putting it down, picking it up, packing it and carrying it around. The same awareness helps us play well in a crowded opera pit or a spacious open-air theatre.

> To me it is an expansion of the field of consciousness (or of attention if you object to the term consciousness) in space and in time so that you are taking in both yourself and your environment, both the present moment and the next. It is a unified field organized around the Self as a center. At the beginning it has a very simple system of organization but it always takes in both the Self (including the relation of the head to the trunk) and something in the environment.[5]

---

[4]Patrick Macdonald, *The Alexander Technique As I See It*, Rahula Books, Brighton, 1989.
[5]F. P. Jones, *Learning How to Learn*, Sheldrake Press, London, 1974.

Awareness and intonation

When we are considering the balance between awareness and attention it can be useful to think of a percentage split. We can use intonation as an example of this.

Maybe, in a rehearsal, a member of the group points out that a chord needs tuning. Your thinking brain gets interested in the challenge and you decide to try hard to bring your attention to your pitch to make sure your note is in tune. Then you remember that playing in tune is an interactive exercise for the whole group and you decide to listen to the other pitches that are being played. So you have changed your ratio of attention to awareness and included more external awareness. Now, the chord might not be sounding in tune, but all the good musicians that you are playing with are confident that their pitches are okay. Someone suggests that you consider the blend of sound – maybe the chord sounds better now, then another player suggests considering the balance – now the chord sounds 'in tune'. The increase in overall awareness rather than specific attention to pitch made the difference.

You could start with a different attitude. Give pitch 30 per cent of your consciousness and include all the other essential musical qualities in the other 70 per cent. Without the other 70 per cent, that is, keeping the big picture in mind you might continue to struggle to get the chord in tune because there are so many vital elements involved.

Let yourself play in tune

An intention to allow the intonation to be good rather than make it good might, at first, seem vague and unreliable but that is probably the most reliable state to be in. A sound has to be centred and clearly audible to make it easy to hear the pitch. If your colleagues make centred pitches you can play in tune with them more easily. So there is a certain amount of instrumental technique that makes intonation easier for everyone. If all the players understand that matching the sound qualities, including the blend and the balance is important, intonation becomes easy and almost automatic. It does not need so much attention; in fact you are best off if it is a more general awareness. Deciding that you need to play the note sharper is not a long-term solution. It lacks the comprehensive awareness that is ideal and lacks the awareness and flexibility that gives you the best chance of the intonation being good on future occasions. The suggestion here is not to avoid precise analysis, in fact close analysis of intonation is very productive but, as stated previously, the thinking brain is not responsible for good coordination directly. The thinking brain's job here is to be aware of anything that might get in the way of working precisely (e.g. balance, blend, attack, vibrato); then you have a good chance of getting your sensory and reflex mechanisms playing their full role in the process, allowing you to play in tune.

- If you are aware of the various influences on intonation and you are well coordinated, you will play in tune!

Feel your instrument

We benefit from sensing the vibration of our instrument in relation to that of the whole ensemble. Everything feels resonant when the group is playing 'in tune', we can sense the 'consonance' and our instrument speaks freely taking its rightful place in the sound picture that we are part of. That feeling is diminished or ignored if we overfocus on listening. The same can happen if we are overfocused in our vision; if we are glued to our score we are shutting down on overall awareness.

Look on top of it

If you take a moment to bring your awareness to the impression you are giving to the other performers it could make a real difference. It is very difficult to play in tune, in every way, with a colleague who looks anxious. It is often easier to see this in other players than to see it in yourself (Alexander could not see what he was doing, at first). We have all had that experience; the anxiety is infectious and the tightening necessary to express the anxiety reduces the broad spectrum of awareness to a narrow band of attention. You can help the whole ensemble play in tune by being sanguine in demeanour (look cool!).

Our emotions affect our awareness

When we feel calm and confident it is relatively easy to have an expanded field of attention. We find this more difficult if we are anxious or fearful. We may feel we need to 'control' specific outside circumstances or other people; this tends to reduce our sense of presence and awareness in general. Ideally we are happy to be present and able to direct our attention to what is needed at that moment, taking responsibility for our reactions.

- Allow yourself to access your reflex responses.
- Be aware of trying to make things happen directly.
- Let yourself play with precision.
- Let yourself play beautifully.

Awareness of movement

We are designed to move. When we are moving we tend to be freer than when we are static. As our body rebalances in all situations, subtle movement is taking place, refreshing our relationship with gravity and whatever we are standing or sitting on. For musicians, it is good practice to check on your breathing every so often, to make sure you are not restricting or holding your breath. Simply tune in to the movement that is your breathing.

Three questions to raise awareness[6]

1. Am I seeing?
2. Am I breathing?
3. Am I balancing?

- Balance your internal and external awareness.
- Balance general awareness with appropriate attention.

---

[6]Lee Warren's three questions (Lee is a magician and Alexander teacher).

- Let awareness of your environment bring you into presence.
- Be aware of your movement, it's keeping you healthy.
- Keep an occasional eye on your breathing, it's good for you.
- Let yourself play well.

Student quotes

When I just let go 'into the moment' (not getting ahead of myself) I find myself balanced and all parts moving together.

Claire Thirion, cellist

This evening we had our Rachmaninov/Prokofiev concert. I greatly enjoyed myself, but I felt like it was a success from a more personal point of view because I was able to really be in the present whilst performing and wasn't bothered by any of the usual internal dialogues. I feel like a lot of the work I have done over the past few weeks is slowly beginning to take effect – for instance, I remember one particularly frenetic passage in the Rachmaninov where I had trained myself during rehearsals to focus on my breathing rather than getting caught up in the notes, that I managed to remember in performance. Obviously I realize this is only the very beginning of my Alexander Technique journey.

Brigid Coleridge, violinist

PART THREE

Tuning your instrument

CHAPTER NINE

Body Mapping

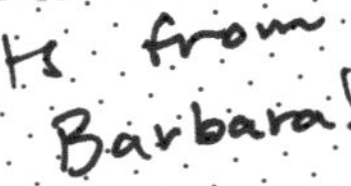

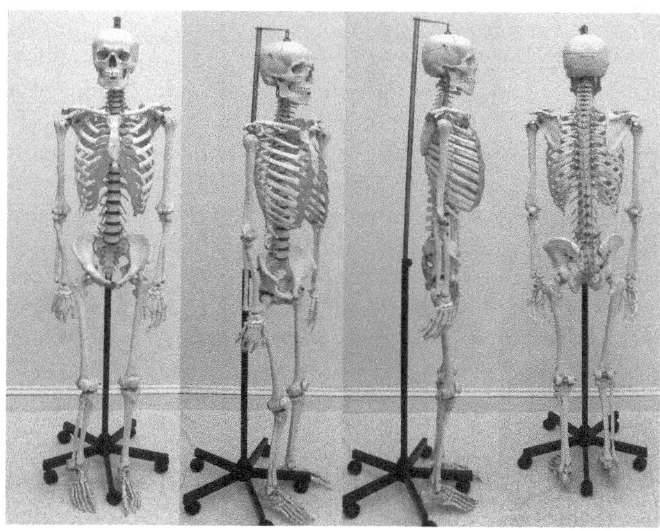

Body Mapping is the conscious correction and refining of one's Body Map to produce efficient, graceful movement. Body Mapping, over time with application, allows any musician to play like a natural.[1]

Barbara Conable

[1]Conable, *What Every Musician Needs to Know About the Body.*

The Body Map is one's self-representation in one's own brain. If the Body Map is accurate, movement is good. If the Body Map is inaccurate or inadequate, movement is inefficient and injury-producing.[2]

Barbara Conable

Body Mapping is an approach to understanding the way your body functions best. It involves anatomy but not in a dry academic way. You learn with your mind and body, especially your nervous system, how you are designed to move. It involves recognizing 'faulty sensory awareness', which has a close relationship with Body Mapping.

William Conable, a cello professor and Alexander teacher discovered the significance of a correct 'body map' when trying to help a very musically talented cello student. Her playing was awkward and did not respond to his suggestions of how to improve in the way he expected. He experimented at home, using a mirror, playing in a way that looked like her. He felt he was trying to move at places where his body was not designed to articulate (at the joints). On asking her, at the next lesson, where various joints in her body were, he found she had an inaccurate idea of her skeletal anatomy. They worked together to develop a clear sense of where her joints were, that is, where she was designed to move. From that point on, she made progress with her playing in the way William Conable had expected.

How Body Mapping was formulated

William Conable discussed his findings with his wife, Barbara, and they looked into the implications of his research. They formulated an approach that is now accepted widely as part of the Alexander Technique – it is a way of developing 'accurate sensory awareness'. The thesis is we always attempt to move according to our body

---

[2]Barbara Conable, *What Every Musician Needs to Know About the Body*, Andover Press, Portland, 2000.

map (our conception, usually subconscious, of where we should move). If the map is correct, all works well and coordination is good. If there is a discrepancy between the two, we compromise the accuracy and fluency of our gestures.

Best and worst case scenarios

The best scenario is when we have a clear idea of our body's design and it is accurate. The worst case scenario is when we have a clear idea but it is wrong. Interestingly, there are variations within the grey area between the two ends of the spectrum. If we try to sense where joints are and then estimate; when our estimate is accurate, things will be working pretty well and when we are inaccurate our coordination is less reliable. What we are dealing with is 'accurate or Faulty Sensory Perception'. The Faulty Sensory Perception when playing a musical instrument or singing can often come from lack of clarity about our skeletal structure.

The work that develops after discovering an inaccurate body map has to be psychophysical. An improved academic knowledge is not enough. We have to have an accurate sensory awareness of where our head, arms, legs, pelvis, ribs, and the like are, and how they move in relation to each other. It is very helpful to have an Alexander teacher's hands on to help locate and facilitate movement at joints that we are not clear about.

There are many Alexander teachers who include Body Mapping in their teaching and there are books written about Body Mapping for musicians. The obvious one to start with is Barbara Conable's, *What Every Musician Needs to Know about the Body.*[3] We consider this book compulsory reading for music students. There are more specific body mapping books for performers, for example, violin, piano/organ, flute. They are based on the same principles but written by students of Body Mapping who play the different instruments.

---

[3]Conable, *What Every Musician Needs to Know About the Body.*

Ask questions to improve your map

It is a very good idea to establish the accuracy of your own body map by asking yourself the following basic questions to start with:

- Where does your head balance on top of your spine?
- Where are your ankle joints?
- Where do your hip joints fit in the picture?
- Do you bend at your hips or higher up, at your waist?
- Do you know where your sitting bones are?
- Do you balance on your sitting bones?

Then you can consider the location of all the particular joints where you move to make a sound on your instrument.

- Where do you move when you breathe?
- How do your shoulders move?
- Where are your rib joints?
- Do you include the collarbones and shoulder blades in your arm-map?
- Where do your arms join onto your body?
- How do your lower arms move when you turn your hands over?
- Where are your wrist bones?
- How do your hands join onto your arms?
- Do you know about the joints in your fingers?

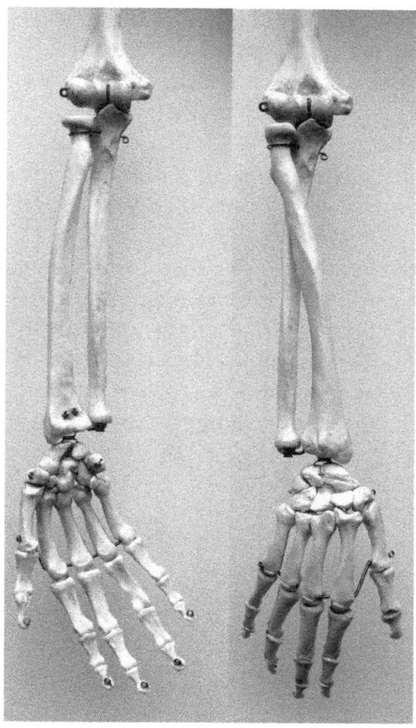

The bones in the hand and lower arm

When you see the bones, it is obvious where the fingers begin (at the wrist).

You can see the eight bones that are the wrist.

The hand joins onto the bone on the thumb side of the arm (the Radius).

Hand and arm – Body Mapping

You can check in an anatomy book how accurate your ideas are, but remember to enjoy the psychophysical reality of what you discover, that makes the knowledge useful.

Musicians move their body to make a living

Barbara Conable points out that it is sometimes a well-kept secret that you have to move to make a sound on a musical instrument, so you move to make a living, like a dancer or an actor. The result of an accurate body map is that you will have the basis for good coordination when you are learning to play a musical instrument.

If you have developed your instrumental technique with an inaccurate map, you will not be realizing your full potential. It will take some work to deal with any Faulty Sensory Perception because knowing academically where a joint lives is quite different to knowing with your mind and body.

When your map becomes updated with the reality of your body, you will notice that playing becomes easier, more pleasurable and more accurate.

Many musicians injure themselves when playing their instrument. Body Mapping can be part of the solution for many sufferers. To give one example; musicians with RSI in the lower arms will usually find their solution when they understand (psychophysically) the way the radius moves diagonally across the ulna, when turning their palms down. They learn to stop using the upper arm to turn the hand over.

EXPERIMENT

Lay your forearms on a table and turn your hands over – if you see your hands flop over one side and then the other of your little fingers, with your little fingers staying more or less where they are, the healthy pivoting movement is happening. The picture is not good if your hands remain, more or less, where they are with the little fingers sliding from side to side; you will be using the upper arm to make the turns.

Now st[illegible] [illegible]ur lower arms at a right angle [illegible] your palms up. Turn the palms over an[illegible] [illegible]movement takes place. If your elbows stay more or [illegible] they are, things are going well. If things are not going so well, you might notice your elbows moving away from your body, moving at the shoulder joints does this.

If you are young you might be getting away with using an inaccurate body map and not feeling any discomfort. However, now is the time to upgrade your map!

Poor coordination is the first sign

The first symptom of a poor 'body map' is poor coordination, which is usually not noticed as significant, we might just decide to practise more. We carry on practising and performing for months and years and when we really intensify our work, maybe at a summer music course or when we get a place at a Music Conservatory, we run into physical problems. We just cannot cope with a poor body map at this level because we have intensified our practice regime. We need to acknowledge our design when we are playing for hours every day.

It is essential that if problems are developing the musician has a detailed look into their 'body map'. The big joint-messages here are as follows:

- Your conception (usually subconscious) of your body, affects the way you use it, and
- the way you use your body affects the way it functions.

Have you grown?

Many musicians start playing their instrument at a young age. If they put in hours of intense practice they will set up psychophysical patterns that become their technique. The body map may well be close to perfect and so coordination excellent, they will be considered 'talented'. When the body grows the body map needs to grow perfectly with the body.

It is common for growth to come in spurts and we all know some teenagers who have suddenly grown and become physically awkward, maybe we can remember that happening to us. The problem is, the body map is not fitting the body. If all goes well, the body map does adjust and coordination gets back to 'normal'.

With a skill like playing a musical instrument we need superb coordination to play beautifully and the body map needs to be correct to have our best chance.

Young children learn new skills effortlessly. When children study a musical instrument from a young age, the same thing can happen. The sensory element of the psychophysical unity needs to develop with the growing body and body map. If the approach to learning the instrument includes free flowing movement and well directed Use, rather than, 'you should do it like this', the body map and the coordination can develop together as the young musician grows.

This work is psychophysical. If you study the anatomy and develop your sense of movement at critical joints you can free up your playing. Even better is 'hands-on help' from an Alexander teacher to highlight the potential freedom of movement at the joints. Ease of movement at correctly mapped joints is a substantial part of good coordination.

Student quotes

I got used to my faulty habits and they soon became normal and 'right' to me. I based my entire kinaesthetic sense on this faulty instrument. I was, therefore, processing information through a faulty filter. And this is where the expertise of a great teacher comes in. Although the guidance of a well trained teacher is useful at every juncture, I now know in a profoundly organic, physical way as well as an intellectual way that I simply cannot trust my own sensory awareness and I do need my teacher's guidance.

Phoebe Haines, singer

It took me almost an hour to rediscover the joints on my hands and it felt so enlightening. I realize that by understanding how various parts of my body move, in particular, my fingers, I can avoid exerting tension on them and prevent recurring injuries that might jeopardize my career as a musician.

Nabillah Jalal, pianist

CHAPTER TEN

Breathing

Breath is the life; and breathing capacity is the measure of life.

F. M. Alexander

Sitting well is part of breathing well

How are you breathing now?

To find out how you are breathing, you can ask yourself a few questions:

- Is there movement in your ribs?
- Where is the most movement?
- Is your back responding to breathing?
- How much movement can you sense in your abdomen (below your ribs)?
- Is your breathing noisy?
- Are your shoulders responding to your breathing?
- Is your spine flexible and moving as you breathe?
- Can you sense any restrictions in your movement as you breathe?

Asking ourselves questions about how we are breathing can often start the softening of any extra tension that is getting in the way of fluent, reflex breathing.

Learning about your breathing patterns can take some time and patience. Observation, Inhibition and Direction are your Alexander tools for accepting your habits, learning and self-development. Making a change to your breathing patterns can make your breathing feel very different; an understanding of Faulty Sensory Awareness helps you to accept that the new pattern might feel like the wrong thing at first. However, by applying the ideas of Non-doing and Direction, your breathing can become more coordinated and easy. Getting in touch with your breathing can be life changing.

Alexander's approach to breathing

Alexander found the best way to work on his breathing was not localized work. He considered the Use of his Whole Self. Alexander had a habit of pulling his head back and down, putting pressure into his throat and onto his vocal apparatus. When he breathed in, there was an audible gasp. His back narrowed and restricted his breathing. His feet were held in tension when he stood to recite.

When he released the backward and downward pull from his head–neck area, his back began to lengthen and widen. The pressure was relieved from his neck and throat, so the audible gasping stopped and his vocal resonance improved. The lengthening and widening back allowed his breathing to be freer and more efficient. When he released his feet, so they spread out onto the floor, he discovered even more freedom in the breathing pattern.

The reason the feet and legs have such an affect on the breathing are the muscular connections from the diaphragm to the spine and the legs. The crura muscles (the lowest part of the diaphragm) connect to the spine, the facia of the crura connect with the psoas muscles, the psoas muscles connect from the spine through the pelvis into the legs.

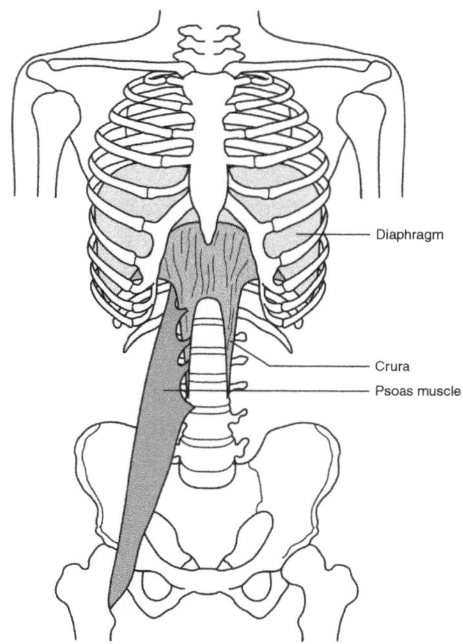

Diaphragm at exhalation

Experiment

Try locking your legs by bracing the knees and tightening your feet – then when you breathe you will notice that your breathing is restricted.

We can encourage the free movement up and out of the ribs during the in-breath by thinking of the back widening. We can encourage the free return movement of the ribs on the out-breath by thinking of the head tending to move up.

- Can you let your Whole Self respond to your breathing?
- Let your feet spread onto the floor.
- Don't lock your legs.
- Freeing your legs can free up your breathing.
- Direct your back to widen on the in-breath.
- Direct your head up on the out-breath.

Habits of breathing

Happily, we don't need to remember to breathe, as it is an automatic reflex process. Whenever our emotional state changes our breathing changes as part of our expression of the emotion. We can however affect the efficiency of our breathing pattern consciously, for example, we can choose to hold our breath or breathe in for four and out for six counts.

We can make conscious choices that indirectly work to re-establish efficient reflex breathing – that is Alexander's approach.

If our breathing has lost freedom, it is probably a result of our emotional state or a misguided conscious attempt to breathe in a particular way, maybe when we were first learning to play a musical instrument, this loss of freedom Alexander described as 'misuse'. The good news is that we often feel much better when our breathing becomes more coordinated and easy. It is worth remembering, however, that our breathing is intimately connected with our deep emotions and we need to be sensitive to ourselves when we intend to make changes to our breathing pattern. We might notice, for instance, that we are holding anxiety in our shoulders, that will restrict our breathing, but we can direct the shoulders to release away from each other and expect a freeing up of the flow of breath. The work is indirect – delicately directed thoughts of change.

The Primary Control

If you lose freedom in the Primary Control, your breathing suffers. In fact if you tense anywhere, even your toes inside your shoes, it affects your breathing. Other places to be on the lookout for tensions are the tongue and throat, the back shortening or narrowing, the ribs, your pelvis, your legs (especially bracing the knees). We can also create extra tension in our vocal folds and at the back of the nose.

The Primary Control is the first habit to address. Alexander pulled his head back and down – it put pressure into his vocal apparatus in the throat and made his breathing audible. His friends told him they could hear him gasping for breath when they went to his performances. When he released his head Forward and Up, the pressure was relieved and the gasping stopped.

Try consciously tightening your neck and notice how constricted your breathing feels.

The phrenic nerve is the nerve that controls the diaphragm; the subconscious brain controls it. The nerve comes out of the spinal cord at c3, c4 and c5 (vertebrae of the neck). Freeing the neck helps take pressure off the nerve and frees your breathing.

- C 3, 4, 5 keep the diaphragm alive!

If our overall pattern is to pull our head back and down, the resulting downward pull throughout the body has a de-energizing effect on our breathing. Head Forward and Up is the Direction to take us out of that habit.

- Downward pull de-energizes our breathing.
- Downward pull makes breathing noisy.
- Head Forward and Up energizes our breathing.

The head's balance on top of the spine organizes the spine's response to breathing. If the neck tightens the head onto the spine it restricts the movement in the spine. Free movement in the spine is a passport to free breathing.

- Address the Primary Control first.
- Tension anywhere in the body affects your breathing.

If we are anxious, we express it with various tensions but the abdominal muscles are often strongly affected. This restricts the movement of the diaphragm, the most influential muscle in breathing. This pushes the breathing movement higher in the body, making it shallower and less efficient. Thinking of releasing the abs can transform our breathing and our emotional state, for example, on the day of a performance.

When we are anxious, we can easily respond in a version of the 'startle pattern' (see Chapter 5: Primary Control). This pattern includes a restriction of normal breathing. We start to act as if a crisis is developing and overexcite our whole system. If we can sense what's going on, we may be able to choose to do something about it. It helps to reverse the onset of startle if you think of the head releasing Forward and Up away from the spine.

- We can work on our breathing to relieve performance anxiety.
- Release your stomach muscles on the day of a concert.
- Releasing the Primary Control heads off the development of slow onset startle pattern, this indirectly frees up your breathing.

To free up tension in the ribcage, we think of the free movement of the ribs up and down at the side of our body. The image of the ribs moving like 'bucket handles' is useful. The ribs articulate with the spine at the back and the sternum at the front. It is worth looking at the angles of the ribs and the movements that they make.[1] A lot of your back is the structure of the ribcage.

[1]http://theartofbreathing.net/stough_institute.html

Directing the back to widen on in-breaths encourages a suitable free movement. There are two pairs of ribs at the bottom of the back of the ribcage, known as the 'floating ribs', that do not join round the front to the sternum. They are freer to move because of this design.

There is movement throughout the whole torso when we breathe, in our armpits, across the width of the back and our front, in the thorax and abdomen.

- The ribs move like bucket handles at the sides of the body.

The anatomy of breathing

Carl Stough wrote a book about his life working with a varied cross-section of the population. He helped emphysema patients back from otherwise certain death and elite American athletes preparing for the Olympics at high altitude in Mexico City. He also worked with performers and people from all walks of life.

He saw breathing as the master switch that is switched on at birth and off at death. He noticed many cases of general health improvements in his clients, when he restored their breathing to coordination. He writes, 'With the breakdown of breathing coordination, accessory breathing takes over and the individual is none the wiser. He may suffer the consequences the remainder of his life and never know the real cause of his trouble is the way he breathes.'[2]

Stough found a high incidence of 'abnormally raised chest', an indication of what he called accessory breathing, in people who were seriously ill and people putting their body under the stress of extreme performance. He worked with his hands to establish a more efficient movement in the breathing body. He worked with some musicians – there is a fascinating DVD in the public domain of Carl Stough working with an opera singer. Before the work the singer sounds very good; he also looks fit and in great shape. After the work, where you see a noticeable release in the chest, there is more resonance and there are extra overtones in his sound.

---

[2]Carl Stough and Reece Stough, *Dr. Breath: The Story of Breathing Coordination*, Stough Institute. New York, 1981, p. 220.

The message here is: it is easy to lift the front of the ribcage when you try hard to breathe more deeply. A clearer idea of the anatomy helps musicians to improve their breathing pattern. The idea is to understand the movements that are designed into the system, and let them happen.

- Don't lift the chest in an effort to breathe deeper.
- Release your ribcage when breathing out.
- Let there be plenty of movement in the thorax.

How the diaphragm does its job

The diaphragm is the main muscle of breathing that lies horizontally in the torso separating the lungs from the abdomen. It is higher in the front than the back. Your lungs and heart are above and your abdominal viscera below the diaphragm. The diaphragm works automatically; it is triggered into action by a subconscious part of the brain that monitors the ratio of carbon dioxide to oxygen in your blood. When you need more oxygen, you take the next breath. You cannot directly feel or decide to move the diaphragm; you can feel some of the responses to the moving diaphragm in other parts of the body and you can affect its movement indirectly.

The diaphragm flattens, drawing the lungs down, creating the space for the lungs to fill with air. It also helps the intercostal muscles to move the ribs up and out, creating more space by widening the ribcage. With this enlarging of the lungs, air moves in. Air moves in through the nose or mouth to even up the pressure inside and outside your body. If you allow it, air will flow into you, with no extra effort. There is a response in the whole ribcage with expansion forward and backward as the ribs move up at your sides. Even in the smallest breath, there is subtle movement in the whole thorax. Every breath we take is a unique breath; it changes constantly according to what we are doing or thinking.

> The diaphragm, by itself, increases all three diameters of the thorax: the vertical diameter by pulling down on the central tendon (the central domed part of the diaphragm): the

> transverse diameter by elevating the lower ribs, which elevate the sternum and upper ribs therefore increasing the front-to-back diameter.[3]

As the diaphragm flattens it massages and moves the abdominal viscera down further into the pelvis. The muscles that form the pelvic floor respond by receiving the viscera in a mirroring of the downward movement of the diaphragm above. When in-breath turns to out-breath, the pelvic floor supports the movement of the diaphragm by its in-built elastic recoil.

The diaphragm domes up when it relaxes as the ribs move down; this is happening when you are breathing out. Breathing can feel easy and comfortable in almost every activity.

- The diaphragm is the main breathing muscle.
- It works on the in-breath but it doesn't feel like work.
- It relaxes on the out-breath.
- Breathing can feel easy in activity.

Nose versus mouth

In an ideal world, in everyday activities, you breathe in through the nose so the air is filtered, warmed and moistened. If you breathe through the nose you will suffer fewer throat infections. For strenuous activities, we breathe through the mouth and nose. Some wind players and singers breathe, some of the time, through their nose. If you practice breathing through your nose you will become more efficient at taking air in easily and quickly.

- Release and open behind your nose to avoid sniffing.

If you are breathing through your mouth, ask yourself the question, 'How are you opening your mouth?' It is efficient to release the jaw away from the skull. If you pull your head away from your jaw it sets a chain of negative events off that

---

[3]David Gorman, *The Body Moveable*, Ampersand Press, Guelph, Canada, p. 139.

will spread through your whole body, including your breathing mechanism.

- Release the throat to avoid gasping.

A Russian, Professor Buteyko developed a method of re-educating breathing particularly for people with breathing problems such as asthma. He noticed that asthma sufferers tend to breathe through the mouth and overbreathe, taking in more oxygen than is ideal for everyday activities. He attributed many problems, including anxiety and depression, to overbreathing.

- Breathe through your nose when you can.
- Overbreathing causes health problems.

Your emotions affect your breathing

If your emotional state changes, it affects your breathing. If your breathing changes, it affects your emotional state. Your breathing and your heartbeat are closely connected, both anatomically and emotionally, for example, if you go for a run or a swim, your emotional state will change, usually for the better. If you are feeling anxious you are almost certainly tightening your abdominal wall. If you are feeling anxious you can work on your breathing to feel less anxious – it is easier to release the abdominal wall in semi-supine because gravity helps. Breathing is disturbed to express anxiety, in three main places, the abdominal wall, the valves at the back of the mouth and nose and the intercostal muscles (between the ribs). If you can use Direction to relieve those tensions, you will return to reflex breathing and feel easier with yourself.

- Sense your breath in your back.
- A lot of your back is your ribs.
- 'Breathing is an activity of the back'.[4]

---

[4]F. M. Alexander

Include your eyes

It is difficult to breathe freely if the eyes are overfocused or darting about from point to point. If you fix your eyes or stare, it usually means you are holding or restricting your breath. If you are bored, your eyes can become dull and breathing shallow. The state of curiosity livens up both your eyes and breathing. The eyes are involved in expressing our emotional state. Soften the eyes to improve your breathing.

- Your breathing is affected by your emotional state.
- Overfocusing or underfocusing your eyes can restrict your breathing.

The Whispered 'Ah'

Alexander created a procedure for bringing attention to breathing through the nose and engaging the voice without undue tension throughout the body. It is a way of working on your breathing pattern through observation of habit, Inhibition and Direction. It is good to start working on this procedure with an Alexander teacher.

> Raise the soft palette (think of something funny so that you smile naturally – thus raising the soft palette); allow the tip of the tongue to rest on the top of the lower teeth, brighten your eyes as you release the jaw; let the air out, vocalizing a very soft 'ah', as if in a long sustained note but not sung ('ah' is the most open vowel sound); listen to the quality of your 'ah'. Close your mouth and wait for air to go in your nose. Now you are ready for another one. Notice your abdominal muscles and what you do with your eyes. Soft eyes help the Whispered 'Ah'.

Alexander was very keen on the Whispered 'Ah'. One of the benefits of practising the Whispered 'Ah' is it helps us to avoid gasping breath in before we speak or sing.

Playing, practice and performance

Without enough oxygen we cannot think straight, our muscles cannot work strongly or accurately, in fact we cannot expect anything in our body to work well. If we breathe out efficiently we set up the conditions in our body for the next efficient in-breath. Our performance improves when we breathe well and Alexander work helps us to do that.

The work we do on breathing *is not* 'remembering to take deep breaths'. If you want your breathing to be efficient, allow it to happen. As with all Alexander work, we are looking for anything that is stopping the ideal thing happening and endeavouring to use Inhibition and Direction to release out of the restricting pattern. We can see it as 'unlearning' the pattern that we have developed to reveal the reliable reflex breathing that is programmed into us.

- Good breathing is not something that you 'do', more something that happens to you when you don't get in the way; it is a 'reflex activity'.

How much breath for singing and playing a wind instrument?

If you are a singer or wind player you will develop the understanding of how much air you need for the next phrase. Having too much air left at the next breathing opportunity creates a problem with the next in-breath. Remember it is good to breathe out efficiently because it sets up a good in-breath. A certain amount of internal air pressure is required for playing a wind instrument or singing but be careful of simply tanking up to capacity whatever the length of the phrase.

As your skill develops you will learn to allow yourself to breathe according to need, just like you do in all other activities. You will know what phrase is next and will take the appropriate amount of air on board. When you get to that level of skill, you will probably be less anxious about having enough air and that confidence will improve your breathing efficiency.

Breathing exercises

Many musicians do their 'breathing exercises'. There is potentially a great deal of benefit to be gained from a breathing exercise but it is essential that you exercise mindfully. It is the way that you do an exercise that will make it useful or not. If you do your breathing exercises badly they could be counter-productive. Consider your Use when performing your breathing exercises. It is a common habit to pull down on the out-breath.

How is your Primary Control? Is the head being allowed to rebalance itself or are you tightening your neck muscles and clamping your head down onto your spine? Are you allowing your spine to be flexible? Are you creating unnecessary tension in your abdominal muscles? Are you adding tension to your throat? Can you stay aware of your environment when you are doing your exercises? Are you balanced and comfortable?

- Remember your Use when you practise breathing exercises.
- Are you thinking 'up' or 'down' when you breathe out?
- Alexander considered his procedure, 'the Whispered "Ah"' the best possible breathing exercise.

Don't hold your breath

After you breathe in it is healthy to breathe out. The oxygen is absorbed into the blood immediately so holding your breath in does not give you any extra oxygen. If there is a pause in the cycle it is most healthy if it is after the out-breath not after the in-breath.

- If in doubt breathe out!

Most musicians who hold or restrict their breath have problems keeping a clearly felt sense of the tempo and their rhythm suffers. If those problems are familiar to you, it is worth including noticing your breathing in your practice.

If you are a percussionist or string player you will be able to play your instrument and hold your breath at the same time. Although this is possible, for a short time, it is never a good idea. Breath holding is a sign of anxiety or lack of confidence. Look out for holding or restricting your breath just before a large leap in pitch, in fact anything you find yourself thinking is 'difficult'. Another favourite time to hold the breath is when you have a critical entry, especially if it is technically tricky. Allowing your breath to flow, builds your confidence.

- Suspending or restricting your breath is not a good idea.

Some final thoughts on breathing

Space to breath

To take air into your body there needs to be space. If someone has a deficit in their oxygen level they need space to take in air. If you are full of carbon dioxide you have no room for taking in air. When someone is struggling for oxygen, they are almost always full up with carbon dioxide. They need to breathe out first. Double reed players have this challenge because their instrument does not require so much air to sustain long phrases. We often hear them breathing out before taking the next in-breath.

In the manner of the music

If you are a wind player, taking a breath in the manner of the passage that you are about to play is good, so long as you acknowledge the design of the human body and consider your Use. Remember that, 'the way you use your body affects the way it functions'. If you are about to play with an accent a faster intake of breath is appropriate; a discreet entry is easier after a slow intake. Whether it is a fast or slow breath, you can use Direction of the whole body to make it more efficient.

Leading an entry

If you are leading an entry, there is a great temptation to change your breathing and make it strongly audible and more dramatic. It is worth practising leading gestures conscious of your breathing. The way we make our breathing audible requires extra tension. It is better to make the leading gesture entirely visual, bearing in mind that you want to be in good shape for playing at the moment of leading.

- Make leading gestures visual and breathe well while you make them.

Losing mental focus

If you are a wind player you will find that you have trouble staying mentally focused when you are running out of oxygen. Being full of carbon dioxide is not a substitute for oxygen. Allowing the balance of gases to normalize when you are not playing, for example, during rests, is vital. Make sure you are allowing free reflex breathing to take place. Check up on your abdominal muscles; you need them to work for playing but not for resting. Check up on the Primary Control. Are you balancing on the chair? What are you doing with your eyes? Are you tightening your eyes to hang on to your place in the music? If you are, you will affect your natural ability to rebalance your oxygen to carbon dioxide ratio and you will be more likely to lose your place in the music.

- Stay alert by breathing freely.

Keep calm and carry on

Whatever is happening when you play your instrument, the emotional state that guarantees disaster is *panic*. Your breathing becomes unreliable, either stopping or rapid gasping; you lose sense of tempo, intonation, rhythm, style, and you make loads of mistakes. You cannot be panicking if you carry on breathing normally; the two are mutually exclusive.

- Put the conditions of ease in your breathing and you will not panic.

A brief resume of Alexander's approach

Alexander's approach is to release your feet onto the floor, send your head Forward and Up in such a way that the back lengthens and widens. Notice your freely balancing body moving as you breathe. Whether you are using your voice or not, look for freedom in your jaw, tongue and throat. Notice the space at the back of your mouth that adds freedom to the in-breath and resonance to your voice. Allow your ribcage to move freely at the joints by avoiding any restrictive tension in the abs and between the ribs. Keep a twinkle in your eye and practise the Whispered 'Ah'.

Student quotes

I hold a lot of tension in my body through locking my knees. This is related to the idea of me trying to ground my support but actually all it does is reduces the flexibility of the top of my body inhibiting how easily I can take in air. This relates to my other issue of my back being curved due to my hips being placed too far forward, causing an incredible amount of tension in the area where I am supposed to take in most of my air as a singer. Also by allowing myself to release tension from my shoulders and in general make my stance freer and loose I was able to encourage more natural breathing and greater rib expansion. Also I observed how lifting my chest too much limited my breathing due to it restricting the freedom of my lungs.

David Fearn, singer

The rests are erroneously deciphered in terms of musical context when my breathing stops momentarily at the rests when it should be a continuation. This thought allows me to solve musical problems in broader terms as my breathing is consciously incorporated into my practice.

Scarlet Yip Ching Hang, pianist

CHAPTER ELEVEN

Voice

Frank Pierce Jones ran an experiment with a singer. The singer was recorded before and after FPJ worked on the balance of her head.

> *The singer reported greater ease and greater resonance in her voice and better control of her breathing in the experimental condition, and her judgement was confirmed by other musicians.*

The recording was analysed by a laboratory technician.

> *The sound spectrograms showed the increase in the overtones and the virtual disappearance of breathing sounds, after the head was changed.*[1]

Singing

[1]Jones, *Freedom to Change*, p. 135.

We all use our voices every day of our lives and being musicians, most of us sing every now and then; as with all activities, we can bring the Alexander principles to the party or not. Alexander was an actor and it was because he ran into vocal problems that he delved into how he was using his mind and body and discovered what we now know as the Alexander Technique.

The control we develop over the vocal mechanism is developed initially without any conscious training, as children. When we use our voice we are making movements in the vocal system to make the sound. We experiment with the voice as children, and these vocal movements become skilful. As we grow older we often start to sound like our parents when speaking, this is because we have learnt by copying. Later in life many of us get stuck in the way we speak or sing, we limit ourselves to a certain collection of vocal habits.

If we bring our awareness to how we use our voice we can continue to develop more variety and skill throughout our life and express ourselves with our authentic voice, using choice rather than habit.

Four interesting questions

- How would others describe your voice and the way you speak?
- Do you usually speak fast or slow?
- Is your voice stuck in an emotional place that does not allow you to express your full range of emotions?
- What would you need to change to reveal your full and true voice?

We speak and sing with the whole of our body. It is not just action in the vocal apparatus, everything we do with our body while we are speaking or singing affects the results.

- If we are balanced and free, we sound resonant and clear.

The suspension system

First of all we consider the Primary Control: is the head rebalancing freely on the top of a spine that is flexible and supportive? When you are actually speaking or singing it helps to think your head 'up'. The vocal apparatus is suspended in the throat on muscles that connect to the head above and the chest below. The apparatus needs to be in the right relationship to interrupt the air coming up from the lungs. If the head is displaced forwards in space the mechanism is continuously out of adjustment. If a musical instrument has not been put together accurately it often still works but does not sound its best. The instrument has to be assembled well *and in the right condition* – the reed on your clarinet has to be in the right position but it also needs to be flexible. The same goes for our vocal apparatus. The vocal apparatus in the throat coupled with tongue, teeth, lips and the shaping of the space in the head gives us myriad subtle possibilities for speech and song.

Vocal apparatus

Our vocal apparatus is a collection of muscles and cartilage, suspended between the head and the chest. The larynx is a pair of cartilages containing the horizontal vocal folds. The vocal folds intercept the flow of air out of the body and their resulting vibrations are the source of the sound that we hear as speech or singing.

At the RCM in the year 2000, we invited Michael Deason-Barrow[2] to talk about singing at a conference for Alexander teachers, who work with musicians, from all over the world. Here is a small section of the transcript in which Michael describes the roles of the larynx.

> **The Roles of the Larynx**
>
> To begin with I would like to invite you to consider what role the vocal folds play in connection with our respiration and voicing, and to reflect on how a misunderstanding of their

[2]Michael Deason-Barrow, Head of the Tonalis institute, www.tonalismusic.co.uk

function will inevitably have deleterious effects not just on our singing and our breathing, but on the psychological and emotional state of the singer, as well as on the listening state of our audiences.

In the Courses and Trainings I offer I often ask the question, 'what is the function of the larynx?' The majority of people reply, 'to enable communication via speech or singing' – (to which, incidentally, I would also add non-verbal primary emotional sounds such as crying, laughing, shouting and humming, etc..)

- The primary functions of the larynx include:

  1 To act as a valve to keep food out of the lungs

  When we eat, food substance shares the same passage as our breath for the first part of its journey, that is, one tube hosts the passage for both the breath and the food until the food is directed away from entering the trachea by the action of the epiglottis descending over the top of it as we swallow in order to direct food into the oesophagus.

  2 To hold the breath in the lungs through closing the vocal folds against the breath

  This vocal folds function creates the sub-glottic pressure needed to enable heavy lifting, child birth and defecation, as well as to enable the energy for a cough to remove unwanted or excessive mucosa

  3 To act as a protective mechanism

  Most of us are vulnerable about our airways being blocked, e.g. if someone puts their hands around our neck. In addition, the false vocal folds – which lie above the true folds and should not directly be involved in voicing – press down on the true vocal folds to inhibit normal vocal functioning when

  i we clear our throats, and

  ii performance anxiety leads the false vocal folds to act as a psychological and physiological protection mechanism, the result of which, however, is that the free movement of the true folds is blocked.

- The Secondary Function of the Larynx is:

   4 **To produce sound via the vocal folds housed in the larynx.**

   For the first three of the above functions the walls of the pharynx are called upon to constrict and make the throat as small as possible. Thus the larynx is programmed to 'constrict' to help us with these three factors. For voicing, on the other hand, the pharynx needs to release and open to enable the vocal folds to open and close rhythmically and freely.

Release your jaw

When we speak or sing we have to open the mouth and that is not always as easy as it sounds. The reason our mouth is usually closed is because it is generally best to breathe through the nose. The way we keep the mouth closed is by using the necessary tension in the head and face muscles. It is the jaw that moves down, away from the skull, when the mouth opens. It is worth using your hands to feel where your jaw articulates with the skull; it is quite high on the sides of your face, just in front of your ears. To release the jaw, you let go of the tension and use the muscles that are there to open your mouth. It can happen that we don't let go of the mouth-closing tension. Some people tense the jaw when they think and some people smile all the time, both of which can fix the jaw. If you are working to open the mouth that you are subconsciously closing the resulting fight produces poor results.

You can practise letting go of jaw tension at any time, when you are waiting for a bus or when you are talking with friends. To have your lips closed, the teeth slightly apart, with the tongue soft and free, when you are not talking, is a good start. Some people, who start working on this, adopt a sort of zombie demeanour: that could not be further from Alexander's intention. FM was always described as being very animated, with a 'twinkle' in his eyes. When you are chatting with someone, let your eyes and face become animated but be aware of overtensing the jaw.

Eyes play a part too

The eyes have a big part to play in your engagement with speaking and singing; overtightened eyes restrict the vocal mechanism. They can easily be overfocusing, but zoning out or glazing over is not great either. An Alexander 'twinkle' is about right.

The engine

The engine room for singing and speaking is your breathing. A moveable, flexible spine facilitates good breathing. We can use Direction to encourage the movement of the ribs up and out (like bucket handles) on the in-breath, let the ribcage be springy and moveable; there are muscles between all the ribs. The appropriate 'tone' in the 'abs' (some but not too much) encourages movement in the ribs and allows for the most noticeable movement to be in the floating ribs at the bottom of the back of the thorax. If we direct the 'back' back to widen we encourage good movement in the floating ribs and so free up the in-breath.

On the in-breath we can allow the soft palette (behind the hard palette in the roof of the mouth) to be free to move up. It is what happens when we yawn. When we are breathing in, there will be movement in the abdomen caused by the flattening downward of the diaphragm (see Chapter 10: Breathing) but that movement can be restricted by overtightening the abdominal muscles. Applying the Alexander principles to overall support of the body will liberate the abdominal muscles, making them available for breathing, speaking and singing. The back muscles have to do their supporting job well to free up the breathing. The head tending to tip on the top of the spine, stretching the sub-occipital muscles, stimulates the extensors to get into action and lengthen the spine, supporting the whole system.

Natural support for the voice comes from the muscles of the pelvic floor (which are like a small trampoline). As the diaphragm flattens it pushes the abdominal viscera down, the pelvic floor moves down in response. When the diaphragm releases, the pelvic floor moves up. This can all happen freely if we do not overtighten the abdomen, hips, glutes and legs.

The out-breath, when we sing or speak, can be supported by directing the head up; the lengthening spine creates a natural support for vocalizing. This support is a natural process that involves some of our muscles in controlling the outflow of breath. When we decide to sing our muscles work differently, automatically.

Normal breathing gets the air out of the body quickly with very little effort. Singing, speaking and playing wind instruments require an economic use of the out-breath. The muscles that bring the air in work in opposition to the muscles that move the air out, to control the out-breath; this is part of the artistic control. It is helpful to notice if the head is being pulled down at the end of a long sung phrase, the vocal mechanism works best when the head is going up.

Resonance

Sound is generated by breath activating the vocal folds. We all sound different; this is primarily because of the difference in resonance caused by the way we are built, the shape we are in and the freedom in our Use. The main resonators are thoracic (chest), pharyngeal, oral and nasal cavities and buccal (space between the lips, teeth and cheeks). Freedom in all these places makes a great difference to how we sound.

> A very large part of singing technique is focussed on releasing part of the body; the jaw, the tongue, the upper abdominal muscles, the shoulders, etc. So much of what I have learned in working with Alexander Technique is focussed on exactly this, and in this way the work has directly increased the resonance of my voice.
>
> Chris Ainslie, counter tenor

When we develop our Alexander understanding, our whole body becomes a more resonant musical instrument. The body in general needs to expand, but we can specifically direct the space behind the nose and mouth to widen and deepen, find freedom in our lips, tongue and jaw and release the chest, all to increase resonance.

Experiment by speaking or singing with your legs, buttocks and feet clenched and then try again with them all released. You will notice a great difference.

Spatial awareness

If we are aware of our internal space and the space around us, especially connecting our feet to the ground and being aware of the space above and behind us, we can achieve a fuller more resonant voice in speaking and singing.

Vocal tension

Tensions are necessary but they can be too little or too much. Too much tends to lack resonance and too little tends to lack focus. When you are singing, ask yourself, 'can I do less?' The question is not specific but your answer may well be. Simply asking yourself this question may well lead to a change that produces less tension and more resonance.

The vocal mechanism is extremely flexible and capable of infinite change but we can leave our potential underused by developing habits that become a vocal straightjacket. As a musician you will have developed your listening powers. Musicians are often good mimics because there is such a strong connection between the auditory and vocal parts of the brain. If we find we have become extremely consistent in the way we speak, we can see it as, 'stuck in habit'. You can free your neck and free your voice. When you are listening to beautiful singing or speaking, see if you can listen while including a sense of your vocal apparatus, you will be giving yourself the possibility of intuitively finding more potential in your voice when you sing. This is not an academic analysis of the singer's technique. The experience, for some musicians, is like hearing and understanding with their vocal mechanism.

Use your singing voice

Many of us do not feel comfortable singing in front of other musicians. It can be embarrassment about being so theatrical or simply thinking that our voice is not beautiful enough to be heard. We express the reluctance to sing in muscular tension.

If we suggest that you sing at the top of your voice now! . . . you might experience a tightening of muscles at the thought of it. The throat may become tight, as might the tongue, the jaw and the eyes, and you might find you have stopped breathing if you are feeling reluctant to sing. In fact, all those muscular tightenings are good expressions of reluctance or anxiety in general.

Why is it that some people sing in the bath? Maybe it is the relaxing effect of lying in warm water: letting go of the tension that stops us from doing what came naturally as a baby, before we learnt to speak.

You are a musical instrument

We are walking around in a musical instrument that works best if we play it. A Stradivarius needs to be played to keep it in good shape. Singing is an enjoyable human activity that is very healthy when we get involved. If we sing we liven up the whole of our being as the mind and body get engaged in the process. That is why there is such an energized atmosphere in the pub after a choir concert. That is why the singers' table, in the canteen at the RCM, is so lively.

Brief summary of useful ideas

The body is your instrument and it needs to be in its expanding state to work easily. Direct your rebalancing head up away from your feet and check that your pelvis is moveable and freely located between your head and your feet, not thrown forward. If you are holding a score allow your body to rebalance itself with the book in your hands, enlist the help of the back muscles in supporting your arms, hands and score. When the back is working well your breathing movements will be free. Allow the valve in your throat to open completely and think of your ribs moving out and up to widen your back for an efficient in-breath. When you sing aim your whole head up to improve 'support' and remember the vocal apparatus is suspended between your head and the top of your ribcage. Try 'doing' less and see if it works even better. Engage your eyes but do not overfocus. Sense the vibrations throughout your body, waking you up and making your life a greater pleasure.

- If that advice was too complex: Think your head up and enjoy singing! When you get the hang of that add another idea and then another.

Student quotes

I feel there is an extraordinary exchange in singing between the body and its surroundings. It feels as if energy flows up from the earth, and musical inspiration flows from the atmosphere around us to meet the vocal mechanism, where sound is produced, that flows back through the body and meets the sounding space again. The sensory awareness, physical release and openness to the possibility of deeper freedom, I am learning in working with Alexander Technique, enable me to begin to feel these things; even to believe that such things exist!

Chris Ainslie, singer

We become obsessed with the sound that we're making, which ironically we can't even hear like everyone else anyway. I have found this useful though as, if I'm struggling with a phrase or high note for example I become aware of the rest of my body. 'Is it in balance? Am I free of tension? Am I moving flexibly?' Often when I ask these questions and sing the difficult phrase again, I do not judge my voice but help the mechanism by adjusting the balance in my feet or the feeling in my shoulders etc.

Bradley Travis, singer

CHAPTER TWELVE

Vision

The world moves. Let it move. All objects move if you let them. Do not interfere with the movement, or try to stop it. This cannot be done without an effort which impairs the efficiency of the eye and mind.

W. H. Bates, *Better Eyesight Magazine*, JULY 1920

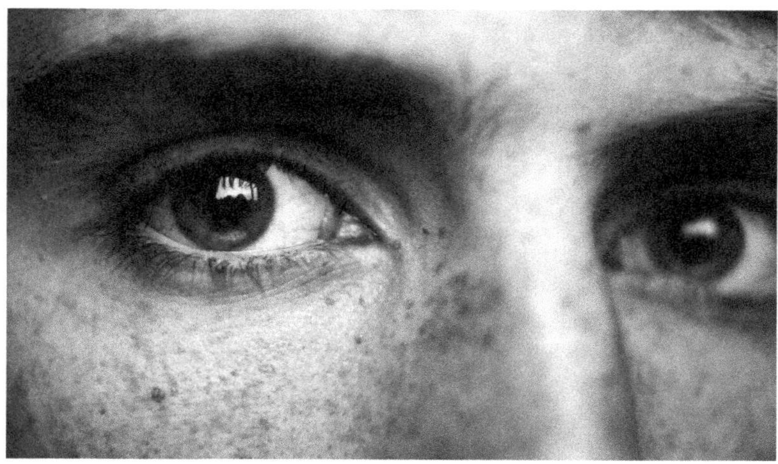

Vision is the dominant human sense – this includes musicians

We have visual habits

Musicians often need to read music and our vision can easily be overfocused on that task. We become more skilful at reading music the more we do it, unless we develop the habit of overfocusing. When we are reading music, we can take in a great deal of information very quickly. However, we can become anxious that we will lose our place on the page or miss vital details if we do not focus hard on the score. That overfocusing on the page tends to tighten the visual system and fix the Primary Control. That tightening impairs our coordination overall and, counter-intuitively, reduces the amount we notice.

We may be tempted to move our head nearer to the music, as if we need to acknowledge to ourselves or other musicians that we are concentrating hard on it. We are better off leaving the head in balance, staying free in the Primary Control and letting the eyes be flexible.

The way we use our vision has a profound affect on our perception of the world, our emotional state, our coordination and our communication. We tend to restrict our breathing if we fix our vision in any way; the eyes and brain need plenty of oxygen for visual perception. Our vision affects our general health. It dramatically affects our practice and performance. Many Alexander teachers include work on vision in their teaching.

How we see

Our eyes gather in light. Light travels freely to the back of the eyes without any effort. The information gathered by the retinas (the light sensitive tissue inside the eyes) is passed along the optic nerves and distributed to the visual brain. If we try hard to see, we are misusing the visual system. We can think of the eyes, the optic nerves and the visual brain as the hardware; our thinking brain develops the software to interpret the information. Ears work in a similar way; it is good to avoid straining to hear everything or overfocusing on one thing. It is good to see and hear the big picture.

Free your eyes and find musical flexibility

Part of the reason we sometimes feel freer to play musically when we play from memory is that the eyes are more flexible and that facilitates freedom throughout the mind and body. If you pick a point at the back of the hall to focus your vision, it is much the same as focusing on the score. If our vision is flexible and panoramic we can easily read from music and sing or play freely. We can include our peripheral vision in such a way that we are easily aware of where we are and what we are doing. We can think of this as 'panoramic vision'. This state of panoramic vision is usually the status quo if we are feeling happy, confident and on top of the situation. If we are fearful or anxious we tend to fix or overfocus our eyes and become less musically flexible.

W. H. Bates, a pioneer of vision work reasoned that if someone's eyesight can deteriorate, in the middle of an apparently healthy life, surely it can also get better. He successfully developed a method to improve eyesight without using glasses. Aldous Huxley, a pupil of FM, found his eyesight improved dramatically after studying with Bates and Alexander; he wrote a book about the vision, combining Bates's and Alexander's ideas called, *The Art of Seeing.*[1] If we wear glasses or lenses, they focus the light arriving at the eye so we see a clear image, easily. The drawback is that our eyes then don't keep fit by constantly exercising the muscles used in normal 'accommodation'. Bates created exercises to help improve the health of the eyes and the clarity and ease of vision. A simple idea to start with is conscious blinking; it is good to blink delicately and often. Although blinking is a reflex activity, we can easily stop blinking if we overfocus or stare at music. If your eyes feel a little tired you can blink a few times to refresh them.

Another of Bates's ideas (palming) is to cup your hands over your closed eyes (without pressing on your eyes) to exclude all light. If you can allow yourself to see black, you are

[1]Aldous Huxley, *The Art of Seeing*, Chatto & Windus, London, 1957.

letting go of unproductive tension. There is a good book describing Bates's approach by Harry Benjamin, *Better Sight Without Glasses*.[2]

- Blink and breathe to freshen up your eyes.
- Try palming if you are feeling overwhelmed.

Panoramic vision

As you develop panoramic vision your optic nerves become more flexible, the opposite of what happens if you stare or overfocus on something. The optic nerves attach to the lower part of the brain, where we process the coordination of our chosen and habitual movements.

Peter Grunwald[3] (a specialist Alexander and vision teacher) advocates 'panoramic vision', that is, seeing the whole picture of your present environment. 'Panoramic' includes height, width and depth. It also puts you in touch with movement in your environment. You will usually choose something for particular focus but that is ideally a small part of the big picture in your visual awareness. As musicians we often read musical scores when we are playing. The music can be your chosen focus but balancing your focus on the music, with an awareness of your colleagues including the conductor, the audience, the room that you are in and your instrument, will keep you and your playing flexible and in touch with the sound world that you are part of.

- Allow yourself to see panoramically.

How much to focus?

Peter Grunwald suggests a division of 5 per cent detailed focus to 95 per cent general awareness; that matches the proportion of the retina that is designed for crystal clear vision (5%) and overall perspective (95%). The 5 per cent is the 'fovea centralis', it is an

---

[2]Harry Benjamin, *Better Sight Without Glasses*, Thorsons Publishers, Wellingborough, 1974.
[3]Peter Grunwald, *Eyebody*, Eyebody Press, Auckland, 2004.

especially intense patch of light sensitive cells in the middle at the back of the retina. The rest of the retina has a less intense concentration of light sensitive cells and receives light from more oblique angles; this peripheral vision is not crystal clear but is just what we need for easily creating the big picture (our visual sense of the world around us).

That division is similar to Frank Pierce Jones's[4] idea of attention and awareness (the spotlight on a partially lit stage). In terms of hearing, it would be like hearing an oboe solo but continuing to hear the rest of the orchestra playing at the same time.

The idea is not to 'try hard' to focus on everything: that would be stressful. It is more to allow yourself to appreciate what you can see without making a special effort. Experiment with noticing the white paper behind the notes on the page. You might find the notes and musical Directions becoming more alive and three dimensional: this is a good sign. It might be happening to the words as you read this book!

Where should we be looking?

When reading music there is one place we should rarely be focusing – the note or notes we are playing! We can make use of looking in different places on the score, usually ahead to prepare for what is coming soon. It may be a change of key or tempo or the 'arrival of the recapitulation'. We may go back a bar or two, in the score, while playing in a rehearsal to see if, 'that really should have been a B natural'! We will have little problem carrying on playing while we glance back. Music is represented by symbols that make deciphering it almost instantaneous; we can take in a great deal very quickly if we don't try too hard.

- Let your eyes move freely around the score.

The music is there as a means of the composer and performer communicating interactively. I am sure we have all returned to a piece that is well established in our repertoire and seen new things in the score. That deeper vision or understanding is not divorced

[4]Jones, *A Technique for Musicians*, p. 7.

from how we use our eyes; the visual deciphering takes place in the thinking part of the brain.

Eyes, breathing, emotions and the senses

Our vision is often the sense that triggers our emotional state. We see something and express our new emotion partly by changing our breathing pattern. We need plenty of oxygen in the blood for the eyes and brain to work well. Restrict your breathing and your vision suffers; fix your eyes and your breathing suffers; if you allow your breathing to be free flowing inner movement, your emotions and vision will facilitate your playing.

The dominant sense

Vision is our dominant sense and the more we focus our vision the greater priority we are giving our vision over the other senses. This can mean that we hear less and lose the sense of our body as hearing and kinaesthesia (sense of movement) move down in our priorities. If we are aware of this, we can choose how much visual focus is appropriate for playing at any time.

Many musicians close their eyes when they are intent on hearing more or they are feeling particularly moved during performance; however, closing your eyes all the time cuts you off from your colleagues, your audience and the environment so it is something to consider carefully.

It is, of course, possible to be a very successful musician without the use of your eyes, in fact we have both given lessons to visually impaired students at the RCM. It was our experience that they had developed great musical skills but they all chose to take Alexander lessons to continue to develop their other senses, particularly their kinaesthetic sense.

Curiosity

Visual curiosity helps keep you engaged easily with the big picture. If curiosity is your attitude, you are likely to be present with whatever is going on; you will have your sense of humour awake and there will be a twinkle in your eye; that sounds just right for playing a musical instrument!

- Our vision influences our hearing and kinaesthesia.

Sight-reading

You have probably developed good strategies for sight-reading. You look at the name of the composer, the time signature, the key, the tempo, any indications of character expressed at the beginning of the piece or section, the clef, the sort of rhythms employed, any obvious changes of pattern, articulations, and so on.

Overfocus is very common in sight-reading. When we overfocus we exclude a good deal of useful information. Panoramic vision is a very helpful concept to apply in a sight-reading situation. It takes a little courage to break the habit of just reading a bar ahead. Let your eyes be available to respond to your mind's perception of the constantly changing priorities.

If you are sight-reading in an ensemble, the normal ensemble awareness can be as useful as reading the score, for example, you might connect with your colleagues after a GP and read the dynamic from the gesture made by the leader of your group. You might understand the rhythm you are about to play because it has already been played with an excellent choice of bowing that you have seen by looking away from your music. So rather than concentrating or overfocusing on the score, you can put appropriate attention on the score in the context of the whole ensemble. Using your vision in this way takes you deeper into the music.

Practise seeing more

An interesting strategy to develop music-reading skills is to open the music and look at the whole page for a few seconds. Close your eyes and see what you can still see in your visual imagination. You might be surprised at how much you took in. Your imagination will be working in the same part of the visual brain that saw the music when your eyes were open.

Then open your eyes for a few more seconds and see more of the picture there in front of you. You will find you see more and take it in very quickly and easily, unless you are making this into a pressurized, End-gaining, self-competitive challenge to 'remember as much as you can!!' So remaining calm and curious, close your eyes again and reconstruct the image, then reopen your eyes and take in more detail.

Now if you play the music, you will find you can play as if you had practised it for some time, you will be aware of the big picture and be seeing much more detail than if you had not revved up your visual perception first.

Your eyes and your emotion

The way you use your eyes has a profound effect on you and on other people, your colleagues and your audience. We all find it is possible to know how a friend is doing emotionally by seeing the way they are using their eyes. You might meet a friend and before saying anything else you ask, 'What's the matter?' or 'Have you had some good news?' There will be various elements of 'body language' involved but the eyes are right up at the top of the list. Confidence tends to be displayed by soft, flexible panoramic eyes. Anxiety can be displayed by darting overfocused eyes or dull, glazed over eyes.

We can reduce anxiety by releasing tension in the visual system; we feel more calm, confident and 'present' as we allow ourselves to see the big picture of the world around us. Other negative emotions can be transformed with the same visual approach, impatience (End-gaining), boredom or trying hard to 'get it right', to name a few.

Enjoy seeing

If we decide to enjoy seeing what is around us we have just given ourselves a liberating visual Direction. Noticing colour, shape and movement in three dimensions is very enjoyable. We can call that 'seeing in depth'. Our vision is part of our balancing system, we are constantly checking, subconsciously, where up is. When we see in depth we will tend to come more easily into balance and feel a deeper sense of our Self – that is a positive state for musicians.

If you find you have got a little stuck with overfocusing, you can look off into the distance and then return to what you are doing close at hand; that can reboot the system and allow you to re-establish balanced visual coordination.

Be in the present

If we are preoccupied with something in our past or an upcoming event we see less of the world around us. If this happens in a concert we are less capable of interacting with the colleagues who are trying to play the music with us. We can also be somewhere else in our mind and not see the score in front of us or lose our place in the music. We are more present and connect easily with the audience when our vision is easy. We need to find a way of being truly present in rehearsals and concerts and, of course, practice. Well-balanced vision is a very good way to start.

- Be visually present and connect!

Student quotes

As I was walking home from the bus stop today, I decided to try out this way of seeing everything around you rather than just staring fixedly at one spot in front of you. I actually found it incredibly relaxing. So many people (including me) walk around thinking so intensely about things and staring straight ahead of them, as if that's going to change something; and I just realised today how relaxing and good for your state of mind it is just to relax your eyes and let them see what's around you.

Isobel Clarke, recorder

It's liberating to realise that in difficult passages my eyesight is not helped by straining towards the music! Some of the pressure goes away when I can just stay back and up and know that difficult passages are just as visible as easy ones.

Nichola Blakey, viola player and Alexander teacher

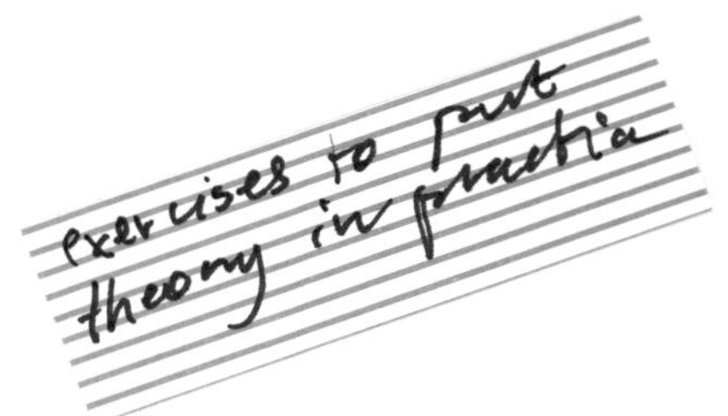

PART FOUR

Stillness and movement

CHAPTER THIRTEEN

Semi-supine

A problem which we all of us face is – how to live in a confusing and quickly changing world without losing our biological harmony, and without losing satisfaction in our daily living. Such 'biological harmony' is impossible without the ability to achieve a balanced state of rest as opposed to the state of 'dis-ease' and fatigue which for most people follows a stressful activity.[1]

Lying down in semi-supine position is a very good way of recovering from stress in your life. Semi-supine is often referred to as constructive rest. This activity is often used in Alexander lessons; with the student lying on an 'Alexander table' and the teacher giving hands-on guidance. If you are working in semi-supine, on your own, it works very well to lie down on a carpet or yoga mat. Lying on a soft bed does not encourage the back to lengthen and widen as much. If you can find a warm quiet place to lie down, you will have found ideal conditions for developing your skill of self-awareness in this effortless way. It is an opportunity to be 'quiet'. It is an opportunity for self-observation and reflection without your instrument. Ten to fifteen minutes in semi-supine can be a good preparation for a demanding activity. After lying in

---

[1]Wilfred Barlow, *The Alexander Principle*, Arrow Books, London, 1975, p. 46.

semi-supine you will experience improved coordination (and what Dr Barlow called 'biological harmony'). It is good to be conscious of taking this state into your next activity.

Gravity affects you differently in semi-supine

Semi-supine takes you out of your normal upright state, where the stresses of life tend to develop. We can often sense unnecessary tension by lying on a flat surface. Lying down rather than standing or sitting changes the effect of gravity on your body. When you are upright the pressure of gravity tends to shorten your body; you have reflex mechanisms to counteract this effect so your body can lengthen in response to gravity's pressure. We often call this reflex response the 'anti-gravity reflex'. When you lie down the reflex mechanisms continue working to expand the body and you enlist the help of gravity that is now encouraging your whole body to lengthen and widen effortlessly.

The intervertebral discs

The discs between your vertebrae can be under pressure when you are upright. There is a tendency for the discs to be squeezed during your upright hours. The discs become thinner and you become fractionally shorter. If you measure yourself in the morning and again before bed you might find that you are shorter in the evening. The discs protect the vertebrae by absorbing a certain amount of the percussive impact on your spine caused by standing, walking, running and jumping in daily life. They also protect the bony parts when you put extra pressure into you spine by bending it excessively in activities or, indeed, your normal 'posture'. Maybe you twist or pull down onto your intervertebral discs when you play your instrument. Semi-supine reverses the process: it takes the pressure off and allows the discs to recover their supportive, shock-absorbing qualities – in fact they can recover very quickly so even a short semi-supine session makes a positive difference. Late afternoon is a good time to use semi-supine to restore the discs before your evening practice.

The curves in your spine

The spine can lose its length by increasing the curves, caused by habitual 'downward pull'. When we are under stress of any sort, we tend to make ourselves smaller, including pulling down; as we pull the head down the spine becomes more curved. We are not looking for a straight spine; the curves are there in the design; they develop when we are very young, when we sit up and then stand. The curves are part of the suspension system built into our design. The spine can absorb pressure on a short-term basis by curving more, then when the pressure is taken off, in an ideal world, the curves will go back to normal; it is when this does not happen that we can experience discomfort, pain and stiffness. Continuous 'downward pull' leads to conditions of the spine such as, lordosis, kyphosis and scoliosis.

Semi-supine encourages the restoration of the appropriate curves in your spine. Let it happen, gravity and the flat surface will do the job for you.

Ellie in semi-supine

How to adopt semi-supine

You lay on your back, head on a book or books with your legs folded/knees up. The thickness of the books under your head should be guided by your teacher at first, but do experiment when you have used semi-supine regularly for some time. As you see in the photograph, the head is in line with the spine; it does not tip back, putting pressure into the back of the neck and stretching the throat; it is not pushed forward, compressing the throat and stretching the back of the neck. We feel comfortable when the head is freely balancing on the book. There is not an exact height, 'about right' is within the range of a thin paperback. Your arms and hands can be by your side or flexed so your hands rest on your abdomen. If your hands are resting delicately on your abdomen, you can sense the breathing movement in your abdominal wall. Your feet connect easily with the floor; your feet can spread out as you let go of unnecessary tension. Some people take their shoes off to encourage their feet to release.

What to think

When you first lie down, give yourself a few moments to notice the state you are in and accept yourself as you are. It can be productive to lie down and not think Alexander thoughts, you might even listen to music, possibly a recording of a piece you are learning, and just let gravity have its positive effect on you. You may feel sleepy when you lie down, this is worth noticing because it might mean you need more sleep than you are getting.

If you want to be more proactive, you can think your way round your body, noticing any pockets of tension. You can give yourself Directions, 'let your neck be free, to allow your head to go forward and up in such a way that back can lengthen and widen'. You can release your face, your tongue and your jaw and let go of any mental chatter. As you direct and give your body over to the effect of gravity you will notice more support from the floor. In fact, you can be very creative with these psychophysical thoughts (Directions) and encourage the whole body to spread out and find a neutral quality. You can influence your emotional state by thinking of being calm and confident and having relaxed concentration; you put these conditions in place by tuning into your breathing, vision and balance. Just tuning into your breathing can be enough but you can practise a few 'Whispered "Ahs"!' (see p. 101). You can register the space around you visually and by noticing what you can hear. You will find poise in stillness. After your semi-supine session you feel rejuvenated and ready for action and your coordination will tend to be good.

Freeing the neck

Your neck is a flexible part of the spine that has many muscles involved in balancing the head. Lying down in semi-supine gives those muscles a break, a chance to rest and gain energy for their crucial role of rebalancing your head when you are upright again. It is good to notice that the book gives your head as much support as it needs. The more you release neck tension the more your head rests on the book and the book does more supporting. When you are lying in semi-supine your head will not be rolling forward in the way it does when you are upright. You can 'direct' it to simply drop onto the books. Think of your neck dropping towards the floor; this can reduce residual tension allowing your head to be supported and balanced.

Shoulders and arms

You can body map your arms and shoulders (see Chapter 9: Body Mapping). Notice if you are holding your shoulders up away from the carpet. Think of the weight of your shoulders spreading them out on to the floor. 'Direct' your shoulders away from each other. Opposition in Direction deepens the effect. Direct your elbows away from your shoulders (and your shoulders away from your elbows) and your wrists away from your elbows (and elbows away from your wrists). It is good to get a sense of your arms full of connected energy right to your fingertips. Notice the shoulder blades in relation to the floor and your ribcage; let them move as you breathe. Do not try to get a result, simply notice what is happening. If you soften your hands and tune to the texture of your clothes, as your abdomen moves as you breathe you can feel the changing shape of your hands and fingers. It is useful to be aware of the eight bones of the wrist and the nineteen bones in the fingers and thumb being free to move.

- Opposition in Direction strengthens the effect.

Ribcage

Below the neck is the thoracic spine that has a rib connected on either side of each vertebra. The movement of the ribs is reduced by the contact with the floor but it is good to notice the changing shape of the ribcage and the back's relationship to the floor, as you breathe. See if you can direct the back to lengthen and widen in such a way that the muscles release and allow changes to happen. Notice the movement created by your breath at the joints of the ribs with the spine and sternum. There is a lot of movement under your armpits and at the side of your body as you breathe.

Low back

With the knees up, as they are in semi-supine, the lumbar spine tends to release. You can encourage that release by thinking of your low back widening and spreading out onto the floor, making more and more contact. Some people find it useful to imagine that they are made of beeswax and are lying in a warm place, gradually spreading out onto the floor. Think of the pelvis in relation to the spine: if the low back has unnecessary tension, the pelvis will tip forward in relation to the spine. If you have a lot of tension in the lumbar area you may find you are uncomfortable where your sacrum (the lowest section of your spine) meets the carpet. Putting a large cushion or small stool under your lower legs can often alleviate the discomfort. When you are working on your low back you can imagine your stomach releasing and dropping towards your back and the floor. Think of the knees on a journey away from your hip joints and away from your ankles. The legs are involved in a balancing act, not being held in a position. As the knees tend to move towards the ceiling your low back tends to release.

Visualize your playing

When you have worked on some of the psychophysical thoughts suggested as examples above, you are ready to do some mental practice. If you put all this freedom and opening in place and then think about playing your instrument with balance, freedom, lengthening and widening, you will actually be setting up the mind–body connections that guarantee improved coordination. Your body will help your mind associate good Use with your playing and it will become easier to let go of old habits as you put improved 'technique' in place.

If you are learning music from memory, you will be able to run it through in your head in semi-supine. It will be easy to identify any corners of the piece where you lack mental clarity; because you are in a freer state, you will notice more easily, when you are in doubt or you nearly take a wrong turning in the piece. When you have trouble thinking through the piece you might notice you restrict or suspend your breathing, narrow your vision, lose freedom in the Primary Control or a critical part of your body for playing your instrument. Using visualization in this way is practice and it tends to be excellent practice; you have a good chance of playing to your ability, in your imagination. There is an added advantage that you will remain rested and fresh for the next thing in your life, if you have been practising in semi-supine.

Semi-supine brings back your skill

If you find that you cannot play a passage easily that you have in the past you can often restore your ability by visualizing playing the passage in semi-supine. Like any practice technique, you have to put this in place and develop the skill. If you develop the use of semi-supine and find clarity of thought and intention, you will get the most from this idea.

Coming to standing

When you are coming out of semi-supine to standing, the head leads and the body follows. Keep this idea in mind and you will take the benefits of lying down into standing. Your Alexander teacher can help you with this at first.

Finding neutral

Semi-supine work is a chance to re-establish a sense of neutral. It gives you a sense of easy, light, fullness throughout the Self. You can refresh yourself so you are ready for playing a concert, a rehearsal or for productive playing practice. If you lie down before a concert your colleagues and the concert organizers usually realize you are quietly preparing and don't disturb you. It is good for musicians to have quiet times; semi-supine is an opportunity to tune into silence. If you include semi-supine in your practice time (20 minutes playing – 10 minutes semi-supine) you will almost certainly achieve more progress and end your practice sessions feeling in good shape for whatever is next in your day.

Pablo in 'semi-supine plus'

Semi-supine plus

Another idea for connecting the hands and arms into the back is to lay down in semi-supine with the arms arranged above the shoulder joints (see the figure above). Sense the effect of gravity playing its full effect on your arms. The weight of the arms encourages them to drop into the shoulder joints which helps connect your shoulder blades into the musculature of your back. The sense of the muscular anatomy of the back improves the connection between the arms and back. This also helps to create a good relationship between the shoulder blades and the ribs. There may well be a feeling of opening or widening in the front of the upper chest and the upper back. The hands are organized, palms facing each other, think of the fingers being free and lengthening up, away from the floor. Sense the symmetry or lack of it in the two hands.

When you have tuned into your arms, being aware of the shoulder blades on the floor, direct your elbows out and away from each other, then move them out and down so the hands float down to lay on your abdomen. Let the hands sense the movement of the breathing in that area of your body. As the elbows/arms make this movement enjoy the sensation of the shoulder blades remaining in full contact with the floor.

If your choice of instrument means it is possible, you can experiment with holding and playing your instrument in semi-supine; singers can definitely try it.

After a little more time in this enlivened semi-supine come to standing and take hold of your instrument with the hands and arms well connected to the back, sense the weight of your instrument and how that weight helps connect your arms into our back, however heavy or light your instrument is.

This sensation can be experienced by keyboard players, not through the weight of the instrument, but through the resistance of the action of the instrument; it is most easily sensed when playing large chords.

Prone

Lying on your front, with a book or foam under your forehead (to take pressure off the nose), with a cushion or support under your chest, with your hands down by your sides, you will sense the width and length of your back, your breath moving your whole back, shoulders and ribs – you can think your Directions and get some really useful sensory feedback. This encourages a flow of energy from the back through the shoulders and arms.

Main points

- Lying in semi-supine is looking after yourself.
- Semi-supine helps you recover from stress.
- It is good preparation for a concert.
- Gravity helps you to expand.
- Give yourself over to the full effect of gravity.
- Tune into your breathing.
- Semi-supine is useful even without constructive thought.
- You can be proactive by using Direction.
- Include semi-supine in your practice sessions.
- The books support your head.
- Support your legs with a stool if your low back is uncomfortable.
- Imagine playing through your music in semi-supine – that is effective practice.
- Visualization in semi-supine can bring back your skill.
- Tune into silence.
- Re-establish 'neutral' to prepare for concerts or rehearsals.
- Use semi-supine plus for the back/arms/hands connection.

Using semi-supine is a way of looking after ourselves. Trusting that we will look after our Self can become part of our self-esteem.

Student quotes

> *I found a couple of books in the Green Room and lay in semi-supine for 15 minutes, lengthening and widening my back and feeling my knees rising, I have to say the conductor looked extremely surprised when he walked in!! On a serious note, it changed the way I perform forever – I was completely calm and in control, and I was able to focus completely on the music.*
>
> Jeannine Thorpe, violinist

> *It is difficult to find the time and indeed the justification for doing five minutes of semi-supine after an intense concentration period when a task is at hand, but this morning it really worked. By taking time out when I was beginning to lose focus (after approximately 40 minutes) I re-centered my thoughts about my body. I sent the Directions and found each session saw a great improvement in productivity.*
>
> Susanna Macrae, pianist

CHAPTER FOURTEEN

Hands on the back of a chair

I wished to convince him that the gaining of control in the simple psychophysical evolutions in which we were engaged during the lessons meant sooner or later the gaining of control in the practical spheres of his daily life.[1]

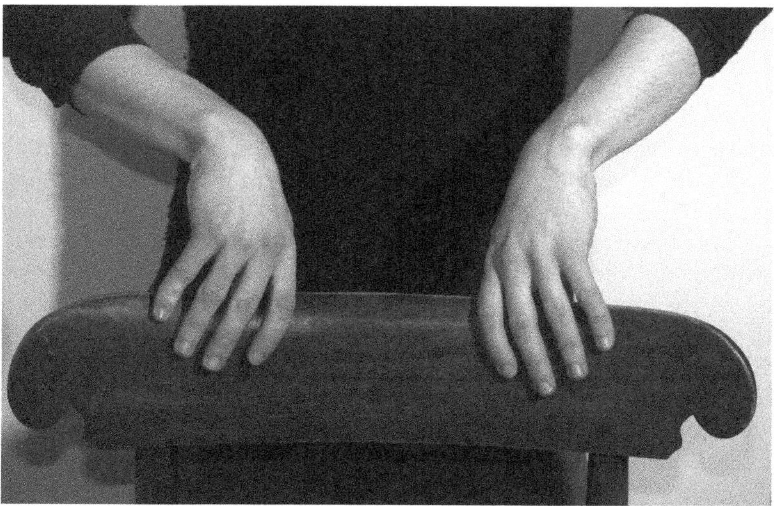

Hands on the chair can be soft, light and well directed

[1]F. M. Alexander, *Constructive Conscious Control of the Individual*, STAT Books, London, 1997, p. 134.

Alexander wrote about this useful procedure in his book *Constructive Conscious Control*.[2] Alexander's description is certainly required reading for serious students of the Technique.

Often instrumental teachers advocate involving the back in the playing of the instrument. This procedure is a practical way of developing that connection between the back, shoulders, arms, hands and the instrument.

Alexander developed this procedure to encourage a developing awareness of the widening in the back that is associated with good breathing. When you achieve that widening your breathing will improve. This makes it an obvious plan of action for all singers, wind and brass players. Good breathing is equally useful for other instrumentalists. If you breathe well, the improved oxygenation of the blood supports good brain functioning; oxygen is food for your muscles and you will be looking for fine motor control over extended periods of muscle usage when playing your instrument. Your emotional state is negatively affected by poor breathing, anxiety levels increase and you will experience fatigue earlier.

There is also a new sense of connection between the hands, arms and back. Most musicians use their hands and arms to play and this procedure will bring new insights into how to support and play your instrument, whatever it is.

Maybe the strongest stimulus in the life of a musician is picking up their instrument to play. Other stimuli that produce a habitual response are picking up a pen to write or a toothbrush for the daily brushing, not to mention our mobile phones.

'Hands on the back of a chair' does not carry any emotional stimulus for musicians. It is an activity that looks at the Use of the body, the setting up of good connections between the hands and the back and improves the breathing. After practising 'Hands on a Chair' you can move over to the instrument with a new intention; to maintain the hands–back connection and feel the overall coordination with the instrument as a refreshed and spontaneous experience.

- If you are practising technique and your fundamental relationship with the instrument is less than ideal you will

[2]Alexander, *Constructive Conscious Control of the Individual*, p. 124.

be creating or reinforcing problems for the future and limiting your future progress.

So how do you practise Hands on the Back of a Chair?

Without doubt, this procedure is best learnt initially with the guidance of an experienced teacher of the Technique. It would require unusually good coordination to learn it from a book alone. So the following is for supporting your experiments with the procedure after initially learning it with your teacher. If you do not have a teacher: read this chapter, stay open minded, experiment and good luck!

This requires either one chair with a back-rail, if you plan to perform it standing, or a chair with a back and something else to sit on. You sit with the chair's back easily reachable in front of you.

- You are doing this procedure to connect your hands to your back.
- Maintain an awareness of your breathing, vision and balance.
- Notice any unnecessary tension, for example, narrowing.
- Think your back back, as your hands go forward (opposition in Direction)

We shall first look 'hands on a chair' – sitting.

1 Now, put on one side the thought that you are going to put your hands on the back of the chair. (That avoids an automatic or habitual response, that would be simply 'end' orientated.)

2 Consider your Primary Control and think of your head moving up and away from your two sitting bones. The two sitting bones connect with the chair

and release away from each other. You have two sitting bones and one head (if you haven't, we are very surprised that you are reading this book). Think of that interesting triangle expanding. Ask yourself what you are thinking of as 'head' and see if that thought facilitates freedom in the Primary Control.

3 Ask yourself the three questions, 'Am I balanced; am I breathing and can I see the room around me?'

4 Bring one hand on a journey that does not take the shortest route, up, out and arriving at the back-rail of the chair that is positioned in front of you. If you think of your hand leading the movement rather than your arm, your arm will most probably do everything necessary and nothing unnecessary. So as the head leads the body the hand leads the arm. To be a little more specific, allow the wrist structure (the collection of eight bones) to lead – that gives a sense of liberation for the fingers to work with facility beyond your well-connected wrists.

5 With flat fingers take hold of the back of the chair in the manner of the photo. The fingers make as much contact as possible as you think of them lengthening down the front of the seat rail. The thumb gently opposes the fingers on the back of the seat back and is somewhere behind middle two fingers, wherever feels easiest for you at this time.

6 Notice, in the photo, how the wrists are above the fingers and orientated towards each other.

7 Think of your energy flowing up your spine, through the shoulder and along the arm round the bend in the wrist and through your fingers into the back of the chair. That Direction through you to the chair creates a tension between you and the chair that can be a very lively connection. This is just the sort of connection to have with your instrument. There will be a minimum of tension and so maximum sensation.

8 This is probably a good time to move your hand away from the back of the chair. Think of making a generous gesture as your hand floats away from the chair (not the shortest route back to position A, whatever that was).

9 Now you are ready to repeat the experiment but with the other hand. When you have made the same connections to the chair with the second hand you may choose to add the first hand so you have two well-connected hands on the rail of the chair with your directed energy flowing symmetrically.

10 If you feel like you have lost the flow at any time or it is in any way uncomfortable or tiring, you should make the generous hand gesture and return to the start. You may decide to stand and sit again to refresh your whole system.

11 Maybe you are now ready for some extra thinking; To connect well with the chair you are sitting on, think of the muscles at the back of the lumbar spine releasing, in such a way that the low back opens – if this is appropriate for you, there will be a lengthening of the spine brought about by a mitigation of an excessive curve in the lumbar spine. You will probably feel a small surge of energy as the spine lengthens. Patrick Macdonald (one of Alexander's first assistants) used to give the Direction, 'send the back back to get a thrust up the spine'; this dynamic language may well be just right for you. Experiment with the idea and decide whether you want to include it in your work.

12 If you have set up the hands on the back of the chair, in the way described earlier, you can freshen up the connections by thinking of sending your shoulders away from each other as the wrists go towards each other, maintaining the fingers to chair relationship described earlier. The front of the chest tends to open at the same time. The shoulder blades tend to flatten onto your ribs as the shoulders release and move apart.

13 The shoulder blades are thin bones with a large surface area. The large surface area is there to make a lot of connection with muscles in your back. This is how the back gets involved in supporting the work you do with your arms and hands.

14 While maintaining the 'connected' sense of hands, arms and back, practise moving the whole of your torso forwards, backwards and from side to side. Then add imagining playing your instrument; while you move with your hands still on the chair.

15 Alexander wrote about moving the elbows away from each other when you have set up the hands on the chair. This is a challenging gesture; it is very important to maintain the correct relationship between the wrists and the chair – they aim towards each other. The fingers should keep their flat, sticky contact on the chair-back and the thumbs should oppose the fingers with a gentle but reliable resistance. The elbow's move away from each other. You will probably experience a widening of the back (particularly just under the arms) that will facilitate good, free breathing. You may also feel that, to a certain extent the arms start to support your back.

16 If this is all going well you can now try moving to standing while maintaining the same connection with the chair. Notice if the chair has a tendency to move; if it comes towards you, you are pulling on your arms – that is not the intended idea. If it goes away from you, you are pushing – that is not the idea either. The chair should stay put, your back maintains connection with the arms and hands and there is a feeling of powerful control coursing through your system, just the way you would like it when you play your instrument.

17 Maintain your Directions and sit down. Remove your hands, making your generous hand gestures and you are ready for renewed action, either playing your instrument or hands on the chair again. Becoming capable of setting this relationship up easily will improve setting up the psychophysical relationship with your instrument.

18 Move to your instrument.

19 If you have to hold your instrument up with your hands the back will now be doing more of that work for you, allowing more facility in your hands and arms. If your instrument just sits there waiting for you to play it, for example, a spinet, you too will find that, because your arms are being supported well by the back muscles, you will have more facility in your hands.

20 It is a very good idea to intersperse playing with hands on a chair when you are practising technique. It can refresh your basic set-up like scales and arpeggios can refresh your starting point with intonation and making a sound.

Taking the modus operandi from the chair to the instrument is, again, ideally tackled with your experienced Alexander teacher at first but then there is a great deal of scope for personal work. The big challenge is the strength of your habit when connecting with your instrument. The more hours you have spent in the years you have been playing, the stronger the habit will be. Being conscious of this challenge is the start of being able to change. We are aiming to establish a psychophysical state of flexibility that makes even the most ingrained habits accessible to our ability to choose what we are doing.

What we are doing when we put hands on a chair is not 'trying to achieve the postural relationship with the chair (although, of course, there will be one). It is setting up, through Direction, a continuity of connections that acknowledge the design of our body. 'Hands on the Back of a Chair' is an organization of muscle, tendon and bone throughout the body, we can get a sense of the arms working as a set of coordinated levers. Every part does its appropriate minimum and the mutual support arrives at a fluent, energized, powerful and well-coordinated whole.

The approach to hands on a chair should have a sense of experimentation; we are not trying to get it right, rather looking for a positive and flexible connection between the back and hands. Standing or sitting, turning the hands over and resting the back of the hands on the chair, one at a time, both together; they are all useful experiments. Intentionally tipping the chair away from you or pulling it towards you, while maintaining the connection with your back, is another good experiment. These experiments will reveal to you subtle adjustments of tension and shifts of energy throughout your body. The minimum tension for pulling and pushing movements, practised on the back of a chair, can be taken to your instrument.

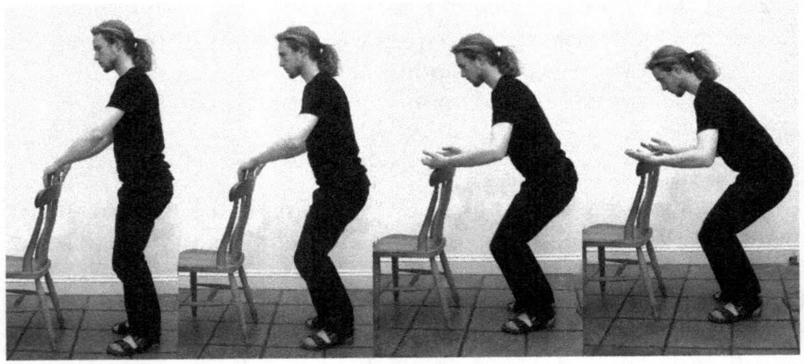

It is useful to practise Monkey when working with HOBC

To summarize: *HOBC informs how you connect with your instrument.* The hands to arms relationship may well be different, for example, playing at the outer extremes of a keyboard or extending a trombone slide however, the connection between the hands and the back will be similar. Acknowledge the times when the connections you set up through HOBC are like playing your instrument (most of the time), and when they are different (rarely).

Connecting the hands with the back will be useful for most everyday activities – deciding to be aware of that connection will be adding to your skill with your instrument, for example, brushing your teeth with a good hands–back connection will be practising making the same connection you need when playing your instrument.

Student quotes

Today I looked at the trees outside my window more closely and realised that all the branches reach upward out of the trunk and then bend downward. When I relate this to my playing I imagine my arms and violin releasing out of my back, upwards first and then resting in their natural position, in a condition that would allow a gentle breeze to move them. This idea comes from the Hands on the back of a chair which I practise before picking up my instrument.

Anna Cashell, violinist

Hands on back of chair: When hands on the back of a chair goes really well, it creates the space and strength of direction that I look for when I am playing.

Nichola Blakey, viola player and Alexander teacher

CHAPTER FIFTEEN

Balance

Because the centre of gravity (of the head) is forward from the point of support, balance must be maintained by

the muscles and the ligaments attached to the occiput. This balance serves two purposes: it orientates the head to the environment, and keeps the extensor muscles under stretch from above. The efficiency of the system is directly related to the distance between the centre of gravity and the point at which the head is balanced. Maximising this distance (the axis of rotation) maximises the torque on the head, stretches extensor muscles and facilitates lengthening of the spine. Conversely shortening the distance reduces the torque and with it the stretch stimulus.[1]

F. P. Jones

When a musician is playing, their body needs to be in balance with their instrument as a totality. Alexander work is a balance between your mind, body and emotions. We balance our awareness with our attention. Musicians have to balance their internal and external awareness. This work helps musicians notice the balance between their playing and the rest of their life.

Balance or tension

There is always a trade-off between 'balance' and tension. If you hold yourself out of balance when you play, you have to use continuous muscular tension to keep yourself there without falling over. You are looking for a quite different arrangement, where you have a continuous rebalancing throughout your body that allows the greatest freedom in your standing, sitting, walking and playing your instrument.

Many people misunderstand the Alexander approach as 'relaxation'. This can lead to a static heaviness and downward pull. This is quite different from the lightness and ease that a balanced

---

[1]Jones, *Freedom to Change*, p. 147.

expanding body gives us. Balancing involves constant subtle movements, fine adjustments that are keeping your body moveable and ready for action.

- Balancing is completely different from being static.

If you are in 'balance' there will be some postural tension that is on-going and necessary, for example, the extensor muscles referred to in the quote at the beginning of this chapter; it will be a completely reasonable minimum. You will sense that core support as lightness and ease – not as effort. In balance, you will be comfortable and your coordination will be easy.

What we mean by 'balance' is an efficient use of the body in relation to gravity. We are not necessarily looking for perpendicular and never for straight. There will be movements for playing our instrument but there will be a continuous rebalancing of the whole body accompanying all those movements, if we let them happen. With that continuous rebalancing we discover the minimum tension.

Balance with the instrument

For playing musical instruments, we have to take ourselves into balance with the instrument. If a trombonist was in balance and we took their instrument away, they would not be in balance anymore, as their body would have adjusted to offset the lifted weight of the instrument. It would be possible for the trombonist to stiffen her body with muscular tension to stop the falling backwards and stay in a similar, now far less balanced, position. However, if she usually rebalances, she would simply (subconsciously) rebalance her body over her feet. It works well and feels good!

- Do you stiffen your legs when you lift your instrument?
- Do you pull your shoulders back?
- Do you raise your chest?
- Do you hold your breath?
- Do you fix your eyes?

- Do you lock your hips, knees and ankles?
- Do you push your pelvis forward?
- Do you pull your head forward and/or down?

The answer to all those questions affects your ability to balance.

- Let your body be adjustable so it can rebalance continuously.
- Use observation, Inhibition and Direction to re-establish balancing.

Rebalancing experiment

This is an experiment for all musicians who stand and hold their arms up to play their instrument. If you arrange two mirrors so you can see yourself from the side and the front, you will be able to check if what you are feeling is actually happening.

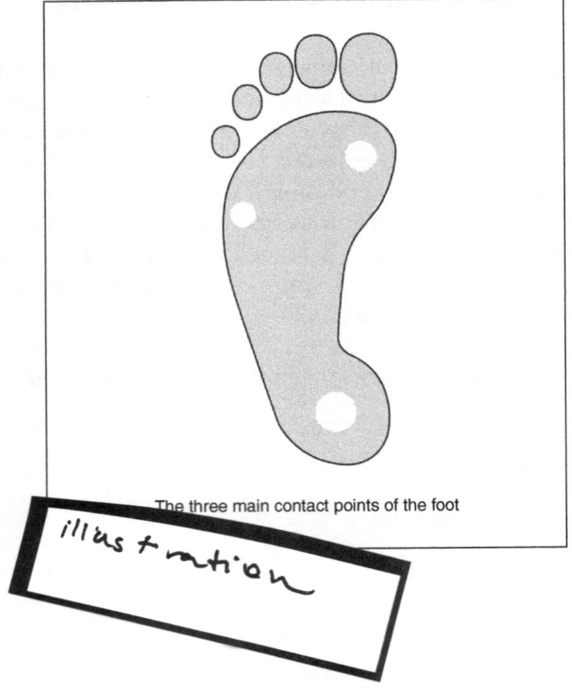

The three main contact points of the foot

Sense your balance through your feet

- There is a tripod arrangement in your feet.
- The points of contact with the floor are your heel, just behind your big toe and just behind your little toe.

- Can you sense those points of contact?
- Is there more on the left foot or the right foot?
- Is there more towards the heels or towards the balls of your feet?
- Is there more towards the outsides or insides of your feet?
- Is there a sense of equilibrium and easy movement when you stand?

- In standing we are looking for a balance that might be described as about 50/50 right and left, 50/50 back and front.
- If that is not the case direct your head up, take a few steps, stop and assess it again.

When you are encouraging your body to rebalance, the Primary Control comes into the picture as a priority. Free your head to go forward and up and the whole body will be more likely to rebalance at the ankles.

Now, slowly swing your arms forward and up in front of you (see figure p. 157) and sense what is happening in your body. We are looking for the whole body to move back in a coordinated balancing movement at the ankle joints, compensating for the weight of your arms that are now out in front of you, not the hips going forward and leaning back from the waist.

The weight on your feet has an important contribution to make to your support mechanisms. If you release the top and bottom of your feet, it sends a stimulus through the nervous system to the reflexes that keep you lengthening and balancing in response to gravity.

- Allow your feet to spread out onto the floor.

Without your instrument

Many of us perform, and practise our instrument, standing. When you are standing waiting for a bus, you are developing your pattern of standing. If you are seeing waiting for the bus as practice time you understand the power of habit. If you have your head freely rebalancing on the top of your spine, your head over your ankle joints and your hip joints freely rebalancing your pelvis between your head and feet, it's healthy and coordinated standing. The skill is transferable into our playing. If we are aware of the space around us, that is, above our head and behind us, we are more likely to be rebalancing.

Ask yourself the following questions:

- Where the weight is on your feet?
- Where is your atlanto-occipital joint in relation to your ankles?
- Is your pelvis free to move?
- Are your legs free at the knees?

The awareness that comes in answer to those questions helps the rebalancing to take place.

Back with the instrument

When you take hold of your instrument, allow yourself the same freedom to rebalance: that is part of your instrumental technique. Think your head up when you are standing and an efficient balanced set-up becomes more likely.

- Every time you stand you are reinforcing your standing pattern.
- Balanced standing is useful practice.
- Ask yourself where your weight is on your feet.
- Notice your head balancing over your ankles.
- Are you free or fixed at your hips, knees and ankles?
- Do you pull your head down as you bring your arms up?

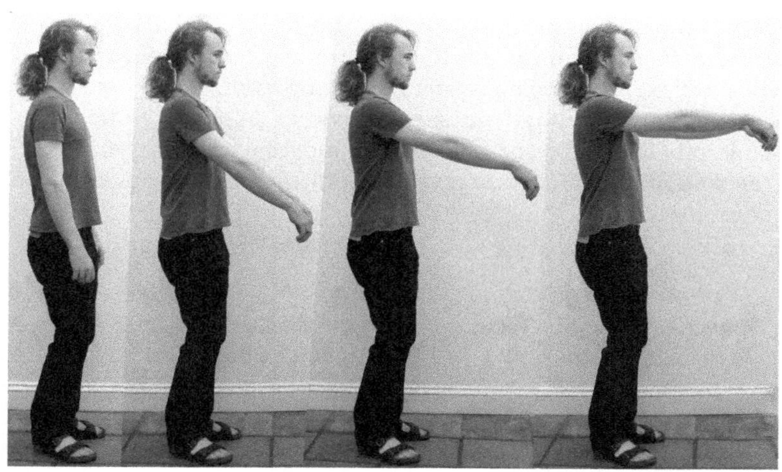

Rebalancing 'arms up'

- Do you twist your body either way?
- Do you lock your legs?
- Do you arch your back?

Now, imagine that you are putting your instrument up to play and move your hands to the place where they need to be; again notice what you sense in your movement.

Many musicians throw their pelvis forward and brace their legs, when they move their arms up, especially when they are holding their instrument or imagining they are holding their instrument. If you throw your hips forward and brace your legs, it tightens the lumbar area, restricts the diaphragm and narrows the back where you need great flexibility for healthy, efficient breathing; there will be more tension in the body than necessary.

All tension is heard in the sound, there will be a lack of resonance and flexibility in your sound, that will be audible to the well-developed musical ear.

It is easier to allow rebalancing to take place if you are not thinking of playing because thinking of playing may well take you automatically back into your playing habit.

If you find you need to work on this aspect of balance; work without the instrument until you can pretend to be playing with your reflex rebalancing system working well; then take your instrument and allow the same thing to happen. Notice that while rebalancing, your whole body moves except for your feet. The weight on your feet stays just about the same throughout the movement.

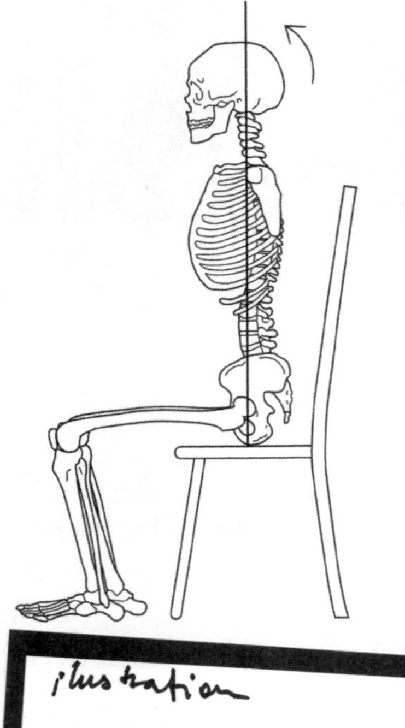

Sitting can be balanced

You can balance on the sitting bones and move at the hip joints when you are rebalancing. Your legs are still part of the flexible support, so long as you do not fix your hip joints.

If you consider the plumb-line, in the diagram, through the AO joint, the lumbar spine, the hip joints and the sitting bones, you can develop a sense of the depth of the body behind and in front of this mid-line.

- Don't try to 'sit up straight'; you will probably lose freedom in the hips!
- Think of your head being free and send it up.
- Send your knees in the Direction your toes are pointing.
- Soften your feet so they spread out onto the floor.
- Tip forward at the hips to turn pages.

If you play harp, double bass or cello, instead of holding it up, it leans on you, so you lean slightly forward on it to find balance: that way you will use a very small amount of your weight rather than extra muscular tension to set up the 'balanced' relationship.

- Balance evenly on your sitting bones.
- Look out for pulling yourself back from your harp, cello or bass.
- Notice if you are twisting your upper body.
- Keep a sense of 'fullness' in your body.

It is good to move expressively

We can find ourselves out of balance for many reasons, for example, when we are anxious or preoccupied by something emotional. If we cannot find a way to recover our balance it can become our habitual state and that will influence our movement and so our playing. It is good to tell the story, not to be the story when playing music.

It is good to move expressively, it communicates with your colleagues and the audience. If you find yourself moving expressively from side to side, allow your whole upper body to tip as one expanding entity. The pelvis is part of the upper body so any side to side movement takes you more on to one sitting bone then the other: that is healthy if you include a reflex lengthening quality in your spine. The lengthening upper body is, of course, just as useful when you tip forward or backward at the hip joints. This effect is like a child's toy clown that never falls over. When you include rebalancing in your way of playing, it looks, feels and sounds good.

- Are you leaving both sitting bones on the chair when you move from side to side?
- Are you lifting the pelvis by shortening that side?
- Allow the pelvis to move with the upper body.
- Allow the reflex-facilitated lengthening to take place.
- It will feel and sound good.

Sitting in balance with movement

Experiment

Sit on a chair and rock from side to side, from one sitting bone to the other. Direct your head wherever your spine is pointing. Notice how you settle a little from side to side as you come to the middle; play around with it. Try sensing how your legs are involved, and ask yourself if your knees and ankles are free or restricted? Now tip backward and forward. You will be rocking on your sitting bones. Sense how the muscles in your back and your abdomen engage and then release during these movements. Notice how you can lengthen and widen continuously during these tipping movements.

You can also experiment with walking yourself back and forward on the chair, using your sitting bones as if they were your feet. You need to get your head going up for this to work well, then you get a lively and flexible sense of balancing on the chair.

We are designed for movement and we are more likely to be comfortable in movement than if we are static. If you bring your attention to these healthy movements without holding your instrument then reintroduce your instrument, it will be easier to avoid any restricting habits you might have developed in association with your playing.

- If you are uncomfortable sitting on a chair – move!
- We tend to be comfortable if we are moving.
- Most musicians find it easier to sit comfortably on a chair that tips forward slightly.

When it comes to performing, it is good to have practised an awareness of the rebalancing movements so they are more likely to filter into your intuitive musical gestures that appear spontaneously while playing.

Tension and work are necessary

The idea that 'more balancing in your Use means less tension' does not contradict the fact that to play a musical instrument you have to work and use necessary tension. To play with dynamic rhythm and a powerful projecting sound is not possible without using energy and, on some instruments, considerable energy. All the well-directed energy that goes towards producing your playing sound will be energy well spent. All the misdirected energy that contradicts the design and easy functioning of your body can be seen as energy not only wasted but detrimental to your playing.

You can discover unnecessary tensions yourself by raising your awareness through applying the Alexander principles. For example, considering your balance helps you to identify the extra effort.

Out of balance – when is it necessary?

Our idea of balance includes the instrument and the environment. To consider an example; if you are out in a very strong wind you might have fun 'leaning' on the wind. Your body is 'in balance' with the environment. If the wind stops you might fall, if you are too far from perpendicular for your balancing reflexes to right your body. In the same way, if a giant gong was removed just before you hit it you might fall.

When we play, we will probably have moments when we realize we have to be out of balance, for example, If you are the player of the huge gong just mentioned, you would have a huge beater to crash on the giant gong. You might, when being asked to play very loud, throw quite a lot of yourself at the gong; on your way to meeting the gong you could well sense yourself being out of balance. When you arrive at the gong it resists your movement, your energy is transferred from you to the instrument, the gong sounds and you get some energy back through your body from the gong's resistance and it, potentially, puts you back into balance. A similar scenario applies to making an accent on almost any musical instrument.

Think of a really great player of your instrument, they will probably be an example of a musician who plays 'in balance'.

- Practise balancing movements without your instrument.
- More balance means less tension.
- Your body can lengthen and widen as it rebalances.
- We use all the necessary work, tension and energy to play.
- We identify and avoid unnecessary effort.
- We are sometimes out of balance for a moment.
- We rebalance in the context of our playing and the environment.
- Spatial awareness facilitates rebalancing.

Student quotes

Today in my coachings on 'Figaro' and French and German repertoire I asked myself where the weight was on my feet. I felt that often, my weight was slightly on the balls of my feet. This gave me the feeling that I was able to communicate well with the audience but I now realised that it can often look intrusive and we are not designed to stand like this. I thought about balancing on the top of my feet and started to get the impression that my weight was evenly distributed between front and back and left and right. This constant feeling of moving and rebalancing helped me greatly.

Bradley Travis, singer

My Alexander Technique lessons at the Royal College of Music were transformative, a glimpse of another way of living life. They were a 30 minute haven each week where I could go and just Be, a space free of expectation and judgment where I decompressed and emerged with lightness of body and spirit. I would return to my instrument after an Alexander lesson and be able to easily play a tricky passage I'd been struggling with all week. That really got me hooked – if I could learn and apply a technique to open up my body and become this free of self created tension and limitation all the time, how much better could my music making be? Over the years, living the Technique and later training as a teacher, the fun question to play with has now become, how much more enjoyable can life be?!?

Lucy Reeves, harp and Alexander teacher

CHAPTER SIXTEEN

Movements and energy

Energy vortex

The idea of this chapter is to bring a particular attention to the movements that might be included in an Alexander lesson; these will often be everyday movements. Some Alexander teachers also include sequences of gentle free movements in their lessons as a way of deepening the sense of connection with the Whole Self.

It is useful for musicians to develop awareness of their movement and flow of energy, away from their instrument, in everyday activities. This can help enhance their energy and repertoire of movements when playing. Sometimes we like to use energized, expansive, expressive gestures – at others we like to be very calm and neutral. It is important for us to be clear that Alexander work is mindfulness that connects to poise and movement. The energy and Direction can range from very dynamic to light and easy. We are not interested in being static, overrelaxing or holding ourselves up.

Our energy can depend on how tired we are (early nights can be useful) and our general health and fitness are very influential. It is easy to get in the habit of using coffee and alcohol to try to liven up our attention or calm down emotionally; they are both rather unreliable and unhealthy if overused on a long-term basis. Being able to access energy and freedom through conscious flowing movement is a useful and reliable way to become present calm and confident. Having a repertoire of practised movements, away from the strong stimulus of playing our instrument, helps to free us up so we can move however we choose when we play.

In all the following movements the head leads the body follows, let yourself start by stopping, tuning in to yourself and the environment and thinking of your head–neck–back relationship (Primary Control).

Here are some more ideas and questions to take into the following movements:

- Think of the Means-whereby, avoid End-gaining.
- The question isn't can I do it better, but can I do it easier?
- See if you can enjoy movement by applying Alexander's ideas.
- See, breathe and balance.
- Don't push yourself.
- Pain is a signal, to stop.

Monkey (Alexander called this 'a position of mechanical advantage')

This is the ideal way for us to fold the body and lower the hands, using the hip and knee joints, keeping the spine easily lengthening and the back widening.

Picking up cello in Monkey

Have the feet, hip width apart, rel[illegible], release your knees forward and away, out over you[illegible]en you can tilt your torso forward over your toes, leading with your head, your arms will hang freely. Maintain the length and width in your back. See if you can maintain flow in your whole body with ease and dynamic power in your legs.

Ilana Machover, a head of an Alexander Teacher Training School, who works inspirationally with movement, suggests starting in standing with the tips of the fingers on the front of your legs, then moving the tips of your fingers down to your knees as you bend at the hips. When you are in a deep monkey let the arms fall away and sense how free and released they feel!

Monkey is useful for everything from brushing your teeth to playing or picking up your instrument; this is how we are designed to move, so that we maintain a healthy back and legs, dynamic arms, and avoid injury.

Lunge

This movement works on the shifting weight, again in a powerful yet gentle way that acknowledges the design of the body.

The weight is balanced equally – on the back foot – or the front foot – useful in daily life.

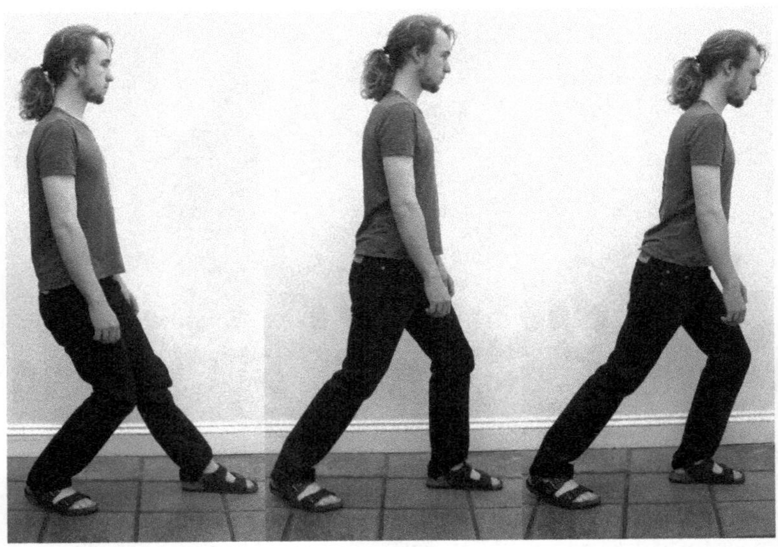

Lunge

Start from standing, transferring weight onto one foot, place the other foot at roughly 45 degrees to the arch of the supporting foot; you will find you turn slightly towards that leg. Bending this front leg, step forward with that foot, and transfer weight onto it when the foot has connected with the ground (play with the distance of this stride). You will now have one foot forward and one back. You can transfer weight forward and backwards between the legs by bending the knees as you shift the weight. You can then gently push off the front leg to come back to standing feet together. The movement can be explored on both sides. Lunges or monkeys can be small gestures.

These movements are ideal for playing some instruments, for example, flute and violin. They are ideal for pushing and pulling in daily activities and are very natural movements seen in children and adults who maintain easy Use.

Lunge and Monkey are very good ways of looking after your one and only back, for example, when you pick up a heavy instrument or move a grand piano at the start of a rehearsal. You can see it as a pension plan; you want to be able to play your instrument in comfort for decades.

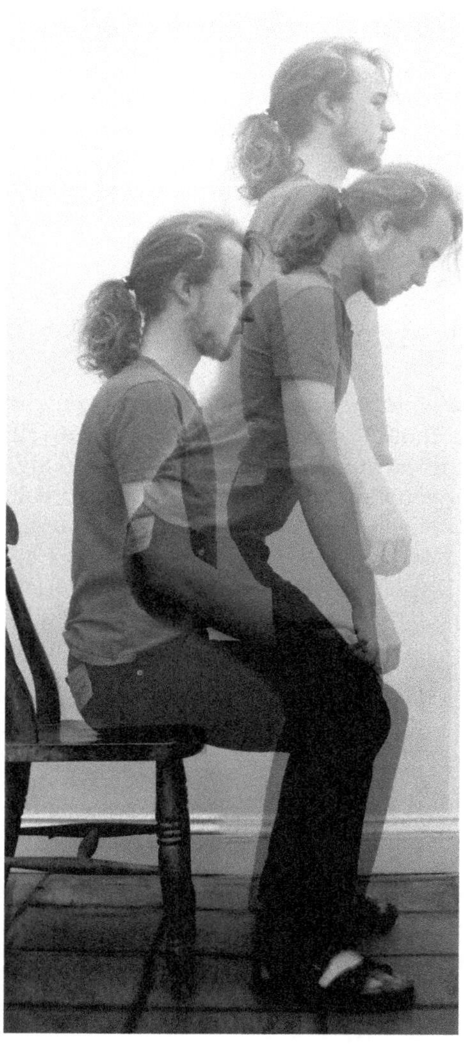
Sitting to standing

Sitting to standing

This is a movement we make several times a day so it's an opportunity to practise being aware in movement.

- Is your neck free during the movement?
- What is your head doing?
- Do you leave the chair without using your arms?
- Are your eyes free to move?
- Do you hold your breath?
- Do you tip at the hip joints?
- Are you balancing and where is the weight on your feet?
- Do you enjoy the quality of the movement?

Standing

- Are you static in standing?
- Is your standing an act of balancing?
- Where is the weight on your feet?
- Are you breathing freely?
- Are you seeing your environment?
- Are you ready to move off in any Direction?

Standing up onto the toes

Stand in balance; send your head up! – let your weight move forward – bring yourself up onto your toes, find balance – then send your head up as you let your heels gently come back down to the floor to re-establish your weight over your ankles. You can also do this with raised arms to get a sense of thrust and stretch through the whole body.

Wall standing

Stand, sensing the contact of your back against the wall, there will be some space behind your lumbar spine (low back); let yourself slide down and up the wall, using your hip, knee and ankle joints, not your waist – notice how your lumbar spine changes. You will feel work in your legs, this is a good thing – don't move lower down the wall than you can manage comfortably. This wakes up the sense of your back, an important part of the body we don't often have in our awareness.

Wall sitting

Find a stool and sit against the wall (see p. 171), again without your head touching and with a little space between your lumbar spine and the wall. Try raising your arms, sense what happens to your back and shoulders. You can then move away from the wall, taking the increased sense of support that the wall has given you. Try facing the wall, with your palms on the wall and sense the opposition as your back stays back.

Walking

- Does your head release forward and up when you are walking?
- Do your legs and arms swing freely like pendulums?
- Are you breathing freely?

Sitting by the wall gives you a sense of your back

- Are you aware of the space around you?
- Are you free to turn?
- What is your spine doing?
- What is your pelvis doing?
- How are your hips, knees and ankles?
- Do you usually carry things on one side?

It is interesting to feel the potential engagement of the back in walking by starting walking backwards. A few steps are enough to enliven your sense of your back going back as your head goes up – then you can take that sensation into walking forwards. When you have practised the 'walking backwards idea', you can get a similar effect by thinking of walking backwards before starting to walk forwards.

- Direct your back back as you walk forwards.

Turning

There are lots of turning movements for playing many instruments and they can get stuck in our bodies. Yet, turning can be a very positive movement for all of us, helping to keep our minds open if we do it mindfully (essential for string players, flautists, horn players in fact for everyone!).

Turning has a few elements that are worth keeping in mind:

Turning while sitting

- Are you always turning your head in one Direction?
- Are you turning your head one way and your body another way?
- Can you do it the other way around?
- Are you turning your whole spine, or just from half way up?
- Do you lift your shoulder on the side you turn to, or the other side?
- Do you lift a sitting bone or fix the pelvis?
- Are you pulling your shoulder blades back, up, down, in or forwards?

Turning in standing

- Are you turning from your ankles?
- As you turn do your knees lock?
- Do your hips tighten?
- Are you free throughout your body?

Turning by the wall

Stand with your back to the wall, let yourself sense the middle of your upper back and the sacrum (back of the pelvis) against the

Turning, back on the wall

wall (your head will not be touching the wall). Turn slowly from side to side, letting yourself sense the wall giving you feedback. By keeping in contact with the wall as you turn, you will sense the width of your back – you might find it is wider than you think. Let yourself tune into that width. This movement helps us to develop an awareness of the orientation of the head in its leading role in movement.

Head on the wall

You can put just your forehead on the wall and lean, towards the wall, keeping your Direction, back back; you can then allow yourself to turn, pivoting at the point of contact with your head; this can give you a sense of the head's leading relationship in all movements.

Hands on the wall

Stand back from the wall with your arms up and palms on the wall, think your back back; you can then gently lean in towards the wall by bending your elbows; this can give you a strong sense

Feel each hand spreading onto the wall and the opposition of the back staying back

of the back staying back, and the opposition between your hands and your back.

Hands on a chair

Stand in front of the chair, let yourself release into Monkey and the tips of your fingers touch the seat of the chair, allow your fingers to curl to change the contact to your knuckles, keeping your back lengthening and widening, allow your hands to turn so that your palms are on the chair – then give a tiny push through your hands to come to standing.

Hands on the table

Stand by the table and let yourself release into Monkey, bring your palms flat onto the table. Sense your back staying back, let your weight come onto the hands rather as if they were feet, then move the weight back, predominantly onto your feet, notice how the weight on your hands can enhance a sense of widening release and the engagement of your back and shoulders.

Crawling

Come into a crawling position and allow your body to move gently forwards and backwards, leading with the head. This again gives us a powerful sense of the back, releasing the front of the body from tension. You can then crawl around the room which can give you as strong sense of the head leading and the body following. It is effective to direct your back to lengthen and widen and allow the fingers to spread out as your weight passes over them like the feet in walking.

Swings

Warming up for Tai Chi or Chi Kung (both very compatible with AT) often involves simple swings of the whole body over the feet. Stand equally on two feet hip width apart, and then transfer weight turning your whole body gently towards the supporting foot, let your arms swing around your body – they may give you a little thwack as they release onto your body at the side, then transferring weight, turn to the other foot; doing this several times you will discover a flow with moments of suspension and lightness in the movement, which can give a hint of easy articulated connected movement.

Arms up

In standing, while breathing in, lift the arms in front of you (palms down) to just below shoulder height, breathing out, let the arms gently release back to your sides, the shoulder blades moving freely. This can be a way of tuning into the hands leading and the arms connecting with the back. It can be nice to repeat the movement with palms up.

In standing, looking up, stretch your arms towards the ceiling, extending your gaze up to really allow a stretch up through the body, arms and fingers – bring your arms back to the sides of your body looking forward and out. This can energize the lengthening of the spine.

Rolling over

Sit on a chair, keeping the spine flexible and free; allow your body to roll forwards so your head falls freely below your knees. Stay there for a moment or two to sense your back widening as you breathe in and your spine lengthening with the help of gravity. When you are ready, leading with your eyes, look along the floor then up the wall in front of you, the momentum of your head leads you back to sitting upright, maintain the sense of length and width that you have found. Rolling over develops supported fluid movement.

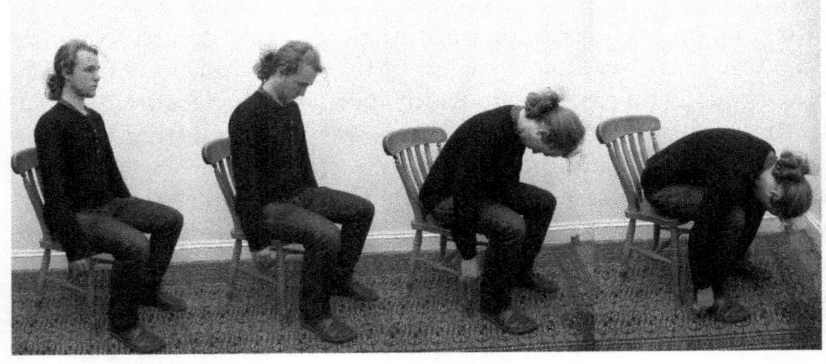

Rolling forwards develops a sense of flexibility in the spine

Our mood is continuously affected by the state of our body. Free, reflex-facilitated movement helps us feel buoyant and light. If we learn how to make such movements we can find a way out of negative emotional states.

- Warm up and tune into yourself by using flowing movements.

We have found Alexander Technique to be the way to become coordinated and capable musicians. Many musicians look into the Martial Arts, Yoga, Pilates or Sports to improve coordination. Our experience suggests that almost any physical activity can be positive but it is not the doing of the activity but the way that it is approached in mind and body; it is the quality of the movement that makes the activity beneficial or not. There are many good books that relate the Technique to sports; running, swimming, golf, working out, and so on.

Raymond Dart (1893–1988), an Anthropologist and student of the Alexander Technique, looked at the evolutionary development of humans and created a series of movements that acknowledge that evolution. His collection of movements is known as 'The Dart Procedures'. Alex Murray (Alexander teacher and a former principal flute with the Royal Opera House and London Symphony Orchestra) and his wife Joan Murray (Alexander teacher, former actress and dancer) who have worked with dancers and musicians and trained Alexander teachers since 1977 developed these movements into a sequence; they suggest that performers benefit greatly from practising the procedures. The procedures enhance reflex-facilitated movement and balance, in daily life and with the instrument. Dart looked at the development of skill and saw the influence of vision, hearing, balancing, touch and muscular memory in all skilful activity. If you are interested to pursue this line of work we recommend the collection of Dart's articles, 'Skill and Poise'.[1] Another inspirational book that looks at Dart's work that is particularly useful for musicians interested in dance is, *Dance and the Alexander Technique.*[2]

Student quotes

Whenever possible, I make some simple movements directly before I go on stage for a concert. This is a combination of different movements, not unlike some Chi Kung, and took place at the start of every morning during my Alexander teacher training. The benefits and qualities of these movements include active leading fingers, good release of the shoulder blade when

---

[1]Raymond Dart, *Skill and Poise*, STAT Books, London, 1996.
[2]Rebecca Nettl-Fiol and Luc Vanier, *Dance and the Alexander Technique*, University of Illinois Press, Urbana-Champaign, 2011.

retrieving the arm to the body, and whole-body coordination so that for example the legs adjust to lower ourselves in space. Vision is an integral part, with the gaze often leading the movement, coordination of eye to finger, the illusion of the world moving in the opposite Direction to our own movement, and allowing the width and depth of peripheral vision – this deeply affects our Primary Control.

Poppy Walshaw, cellist and Alexander teacher

Learning for example to bend easily using the legs, learning to make free and easy spiraling movements of the torso, and learning to swing the arms freely around the body are simple but important movements that can help to expand a musician's awareness to include their whole Self in their awareness while playing.

Florence Nisbet, guitarist and Alexander teacher

PART FIVE
Exposition

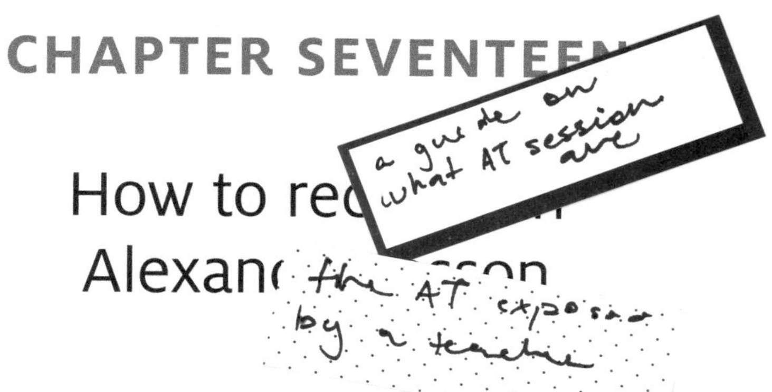

The teacher is only a guide to help the student learn to think and do for himself; – – it is the teacher's job to help the student carry on into daily activities.

Marj Barstow

The teacher helps the pupil to carry out the activity without the habitual interference, and to realise by actual experience the lightness and freedom of movement that come when the primary control operates normally.[1]

Rapport with the teacher

When anyone starts Alexander lessons they ideally find a teacher with whom they can have an easy rapport. It is not quite so critical if you attend group introductory classes. There is a therapeutic element to hands-on work but the process is primarily a lesson.

What is the nature of a lesson?

Michael Gelb describes a lesson in his eloquent way: The Alexander pupil has the undivided attention of his teacher, who listens and communicates, not just verbally but with his hands as well. He is learning at least as much as his pupil. Each lesson becomes a living experiment in bringing intelligence into the activities of everyday life. Lessons take place in an atmosphere free from comparison or competition; there are no diagnoses or tests, no black belts or gold stars. The unique feature of the lesson is that the teacher actually gives the pupil the experience of balanced coordination.[2]

Any Alexander teacher can teach a musician

When you have hands on Alexander lessons, as a musician, you may or may not have your lessons from a musician. There are many musician/Alexander teachers, but it is certainly not necessary for your teacher to be a musician. It may be that you

---

[1]Jones, *Awareness, Freedom and Muscular Control*, p. 14.
[2]Michael Gelb, *Body Learning*, Aurum Press, London, 1987, p. 94.

will be more inclined to listen to a musician telling you how to play your instrument but our experience is that some of our most significant advice on playing has come from non-musician/ Alexander teachers.

The idea is for the teacher to help the student understand how to apply the principles to anything they choose. Some people have described the Alexander Technique as 'a practical philosophy', so lessons range from very practical work, for example, on 'how to sit' to deeply reflecting on how we think. When you have your first lessons it can make a dramatic difference to you, from the start, helping you to get more in touch with yourself. However, the Alexander Technique is not learnt in a few lessons, rather like a musical instrument. Some students at the RCM find the work life changing after ten weeks on the introductory course. Musicians are often interested to have a fresh look at their approach to playing and are prepared to change. That is what makes the difference.

Most musicians find that Alexander lessons make a lot of common sense. They feel easier as they let go of tension and leave the lesson feeling more optimistic.

Safe uncertainty

The student has to be prepared to find himself or herself in uncharted territory. When the teacher helps the student find improved coordination through hands-on work it will often feel unfamiliar. An atmosphere of 'safe uncertainty' in the lessons is an ideal experience for the student, helping them to allow changes to take place. When the new feelings become more familiar through repetition the experience changes to a sense of effortless freedom, a sense of lightness and connection.

Open mind

It is absolutely necessary for the student to have an open mind. The mind and body need to be prepared to change and find flexibility where there might previously have been a lack of it. The work is learning to apply Alexander's principles and that requires thinking. By changing our thinking we reorganize our coordination and our body feels quite different.

Alexander was clear that the reasons anyone might need and search out his principles meant that they probably could not immediately take them on board. The negative habits, that need changing, will include Faulty Sensory Awareness (not sensing accurately what is going on). The student learns to change in a way that does not necessarily feel better or 'right' at first.

Another problem that Alexander identified, he called End-gaining. This is when the student is interested in immediate or very quick results, rather than being interested in the way they might change their negative habits. Alexander found it necessary to teach the working ideas; 'recognition of habit', Primary Control, Inhibition and Direction. Once the principles are understood the student is in a position to change any of their old patterns for new ones.

It helps if the student brings patience and curiosity to the lessons. Their patience will be generously repaid when they find they become more autonomous and more comfortable with improved coordination. They will have to be prepared to think, not only in the lessons but also between the lessons, along the guidelines of their teacher.

Faulty Sensory Awareness

The student has to learn to check up on the accuracy of the feedback that their body is giving them, for example, we often see cellists who lean backwards, away from their instrument, who are convinced they are sitting perpendicular on the chair. It is often a complete surprise when we take a photo and show them the reality. Even then it is difficult for them to believe that their body is telling them something different from the truth because they have trusted their feelings up to now.

Working in a group can get this message across better than a one-to-one lesson because most people believe five outsiders all saying the same thing. The safest approach in early lessons is to accept that your sensory feedback is not necessarily reliable and to accept that the Alexander teacher is telling you how it is.

As you work on your Use, your sensory awareness does become more reliable. Sensory awareness includes the 'five senses', sight, hearing, smell, taste and touch but it also includes your sixth sense, the 'kinaesthetic' sense of your body, your space and your movement.

- Reliable sensory awareness is a great asset for musicians!

Being given a new experience

In the early stages it is very good to intend to experience the new coordination that is possible when the teacher has their hands on, with no expectations and no intentions to repeat it yourself. This is an example of what Alexander called 'Non-doing'; you don't try to help the teacher, they help you get in touch with your natural coordination. This gives you an experience of how your coordination will be when you have re-established the reflex-facilitated poise that is programmed into you. It will feel unfamiliar at first but it might feel easy at the same time.

The changing role of the student

The role of the student changes as they learn more about the Technique. As their understanding of the principles of the Technique becomes deeper and more influential, there is more independent development between lessons.

It is useful to have the eyes and hands of an Alexander teacher monitoring how things are going, however experienced you are, because potentially, Faulty Sensory Awareness is always there. It is for this reason that Alexander teachers often share work with each other, however long they have been teaching.

The teacher's 'hands on'

Your teacher will probably talk to you about the 'principles'. How they say what they say will have its effect on proceedings. They will work with their hands on your head, neck, back, limbs, hands and feet. All teachers have slightly different qualities in their hands. The hands are teaching the same principles that can be talked about or read about in Alexander books but they deepen the experience of the work. F. M. Alexander apparently did not speak very much in one-to-one lessons after he found that students often misunderstood what he said. His hands became great communicators and those fortunate enough to have had lessons with him spoke of the extraordinary changes that he brought about in their Use. FM did write four books about the ideas and would point out that between lessons, thinking work was necessary. FM's brother, AR, talked more in lessons and was particularly good at explaining the technique.

> (After a hands-on lesson), The kinaesthetic effect persists long enough after a lesson to give the pupil an opportunity to observe his own habitual actions against a new background of postural tonus. In this way he gradually builds up a standard of kinaesthetic judgement for himself and can go on to make further observations and experiments of his own. In doing so he has added greatly to his resources for self improvement.[3]
>
> Frank Pierce Jones

> The first time my teacher put hands on me whilst I played, it felt like I was channelling Bach himself!
>
> Nichola Blakey, viola player and Alexander teacher

You may feel tired

After your lesson you may feel energized but you may feel tired. If you can rest or sleep, you will probably wake refreshed and feeling ready for action. If you are not in a position to rest your energy will pick up fairly soon.

Ask questions

It is a good idea to ask questions if you are feeling confused but do not expect to always get a concrete answer. In the first few lessons it may seem like the teacher evades the question or gives a vague answer. It will become easier for your teacher to answer

---

[3]Jones, *Organisation of Awareness*, p. 10.

your questions clearly as your knowledge grows. Your questions will help your teacher understand where you have got to with your thinking. We ask our students to bring questions to their lessons at the RCM. They usually start a very useful interaction in the lesson. Depending on your question, your teacher may give you a perfectly satisfying answer but they might prefer to discuss your question than answer it.

Discuss your instrumental approach

When you have had enough lessons to understand the basic principles it can be very useful to discuss your playing with your Alexander teacher. If you play in an Alexander lesson your movements will obviously be visible to your teacher. You will then both be able to discuss how you move and your thinking behind how you move and coordinate the various elements of your playing.

As musicians we understand the usefulness of breaking things down into elemental parts for focused practice. An Alexander teacher will help break skilful movements into their constituent parts but will also help put them back into a unified whole. They can do the same with instrumental skills, whether they play or not, if you explain your intentions.

The teacher will be able to tell you if you are doing what you think you are doing, or to put it another way, they will tell you if your thinking is getting the results you are intending. This will improve the reliability of your sensory awareness.

It may be possible for the teacher to put hands on while you play and help you to understand habits that could get in the way of your coordination. They may actually be able to help you play better with their hands on. It is important to see this as how you will play when you have learnt to let your body do what it does when you have your teacher's hands on. You will not need your teacher for ever!

Don't rationalize too much

When your Alexander teacher puts hands on, they are not trying to put you in 'the right position' or 'a better position'. If you notice your posture has changed, see that as a by-product of the work, not the aim! If you try to rationalize what is going on, you will most likely put what you perceive in the context of your past experiences, so it is possible that you will misunderstand what makes this new experience useful.

Table work

If you start having lessons because you are not comfortable (this is often the case), you will enjoy any 'table turns' that are included in your lessons. You lie down on the Alexander table in semi-supine and the teacher helps you release residual muscular tension. Your job is not to help but to learn about 'Non-doing'. You are learning how to rest constructively (see Chapter 13: Semi-supine). Often the experience is enlivening and you get off the table feeling 'like a new person'.

Be interactive in your lessons

A good lesson is a two-way exchange. If you find anything uncomfortable, in any way, you should mention it to the teacher. They may reassure you or they might change what they are asking you to do.

Every person will have a different and unique personal experience of Alexander lessons. To a certain extent the teacher will have an idea of how it is going for you but they will not know precisely how you are experiencing the lesson unless you tell them. Interactive lessons work best for the student and the teacher.

Student quotes

> *I started Alexander Lessons after having problems with my throat tensing and constricting whilst playing. I was gradually taught how to rectify this problem by giving Directions to release my throat and jaw area which freed up my playing immensely. By learning to give Directions and release, I have become a*

much more relaxed player and my tensions have significantly reduced.

Antonia Lazenby, bassoonist

At the beginning, I thought it was just about finding a better position for getting rid of the pain. Later on I realised that there is no posture or position in any sense of the words; it is all about the way of thinking and accepting sensory information. My understanding of it changes all the time and so does the way I listen and perform. Discovering the relation between the flow of sensory information in oneself and the musical flow when performing is an amazing journey in itself; and pain has no place in this journey.

Savvas Koudounas, violinist and Alexander teacher

CHAPTER EIGHTEEN

Teacher–pupil relationships

The ideal condition would be I admit, that man should be right by instinct; but since we are all too likely to go astray the reasonable thing is to learn from those who teach.

Sophocles

The student will constantly learn from what the teacher does as well as what they say

When someone realizes that they want to play a musical instrument really well, they look for a teacher who can guide them in the right Direction. An instrumental or vocal teacher is usually a performer or a retired performer. It is reassuring to know that your teacher has performed in the public arena and has established a reputation for playing on stage. We both studied our instruments with performers but some key moments of instrumental discovery were with Alexander teachers. A moment of psychophysical clarity can often put an instrumental teacher's advice in a perspective that helps you turn the next corner.

F. M. Alexander was an actor so it is good to know that he developed his principles in the crucible of the theatrical stage. He became very interested in teaching. During his teaching life he discovered that his own experiences were often mirrored in his students. He discovered some fundamental truths about how humans learn.

Three important issues in every musician's development, whether they are aware of them or not, are as follows"

1. Psychophysical Unity (mind and body affect each other continuously),
2. Faulty Sensory Awareness (what you feel may not be accurate),
3. Use Affects Functioning (the way you are using and have used your body affects the way it works now and in the future).

Students are most difficult to teach when they have poor Use. Faulty Sensory Awareness and End-gaining are serious barriers to learning. When Wilfred and Marjory Barlow gave Alexander lessons to all the singing students at the RCM in the 1950s, it was noticed by the singing professors that students became more self-confident; they became easier to teach; they found it easier to take advice, especially stage Directions; they became better communicators.

There are, of course, two sides of a teacher–pupil relationship. The teacher is doing their best to help the student to develop so they can achieve their (the student's) ambitions within the musical field. They have a responsibility to help the student develop realistic ambitions and help them appreciate how they are developing in relation to those ambitions.

If you are the student and have the Alexander principles in your approach to learning your instrument, you will find it easier to stay open to the ideas of your teacher. You will understand the influence of Psychophysical Unity and Faulty Sensory Awareness. You will understand that the way you have done things in the past will be influencing what is happening now. Not only that, the way you are using yourself now will be setting up the results in the future. Your progress, with any teacher, will be more fluent and easy.

'This is what you should do'

There is a certain amount of 'this is what you need to do' advice that goes into teaching a musician. The important thing is that the student understands *how and why* it should be done that way; then they will be able to use their understanding to keep their practice constructive.

Many great players 'know' how to play brilliantly but cannot easily put in words how they do it. That suggests they have brilliant Use but they do not necessarily attribute their success or coordination to their Use. That is fine until they come to teaching. Their teaching will be good for all students who have equally good Use but students with poor Use will not progress so well – **unless** the student takes on the job of understanding Use independently, that is, by having Alexander lessons. Then the student can learn easily from the great player.

It is worth thinking that Alexander practised for hours with poor Use and then had problems in performance. His practice became constructive when he improved his Use and then his good practice carried into his performances.

Hearing feedback

If your teacher is giving you feedback it is useful to notice how you respond emotionally. If you, for example, find you restrict your breathing or tighten your eyes that will be affecting the communication. If you can remain emotionally balanced and free when your teacher is making a point you are more likely to understand it.

When you have more reliable Use, you will sense just how the teacher's advice works with the design of your body. You will be in a position to re-examine the idea during practice and understand how to develop the new skill. This is as true for musical ideas as it is for technical ideas. With a good knowledge of the Alexander Technique, you can become your own teacher – your practice becomes very constructive. This developing awareness of our Use goes on all our lives parallel to developing our musicianship.

Performance anxiety in lessons

If we are not feeling confident our Use will be affected; we pull ourselves into a smaller space and look less confident to other people. Lessons work best when both the teacher and the student are self-confident. If a student is intimidated by their teacher, the lessons will suffer. If the teacher is intimidated by the student, the lessons will suffer. An atmosphere of mutual respect and appreciation engenders more self-confidence, the Use improves and the lesson improves. Both parties feel happier and the learning environment is constructive. Excellent Use demonstrates self-confidence. We all respond well in situations where we feel confident.

Some students get rather nervous before and during their lessons. This is potentially useful because tackling it, by using Alexander's ideas, will be good practice for dealing with it around concerts. It is, however, important that they do deal with the situation and not simply accept that 'their teacher is scary so it will always be like that!' Being able to unpack 'getting things wrong' and 'making mistakes', without getting too upset, is helpful for learning any skill. To work on your emotional response to the stimulus is very useful. You would start by considering the Primary Control and then your breathing. (For more details see Chapter 22: Performance anxiety.)

Trying hard

Some students spend a lot of effort trying to please their teacher and trying hard to get things 'right'. Some students don't. If you are trying too hard, you might be tightening your shoulders, holding your abdominal muscles, clenching your feet, your hands or your tongue, and so on (you are End-gaining, in Alexander's terms). If you are aware of your psychophysical responses during your lesson you can let go of the extra effort and be more present with your teacher and your learning process.

Flexibility

Teachers will interact with different students in different ways; they need to be flexible because every student is unique. Students are not like a computer's hard drive waiting to be filled up with information. Jeanie McLean, a well known Scottish Alexander teacher says, 'Good teachers make you feel clever' and 'If they don't learn the way you teach, you have to teach the way they learn!'

The 'Means-whereby'

When a teacher suggests a certain effect, if the student's mind is focused on the desired goal rather than how they might achieve the effect, progress can be painfully slow. If the teacher is in a position to take the student through the necessary steps to arrive at the goal, good progress is most likely. This step by step idea is referred to, by Alexander, as the Means-whereby. However, the teacher does not need to have the skill of unpacking the Means-whereby, if the student understands it and that good Use is the basis of developing new skills. If the Primary Control is functioning well and the sense of rebalancing throughout the body is in place, most instructions can be turned into positive results. The student might also use 'Body Mapping' to improve clarity about new physical gestures involved in the new musical ideas that are being suggested.

Questions develop interactivity

An interactive relationship is the most productive learning environment. If the student can discuss ideas in the lessons, the teacher will know where the student has got to in their development. The student will feel engaged and respected. A very good way to establish such an atmosphere in lessons is to ask questions. The student should feel that asking questions is part of their contribution to the lessons. If the student does not tend to ask questions, the teacher can set the ball rolling by asking if the student has any questions. Then it is obvious that the traffic flows in both Directions. Questions bring our attention to choices. Learning to make good choices is one of the skills of a good musician. Alexandrian Inhibition can be described as a state of heightened awareness, when you see that you have choices. Perhaps, the most important person to ask questions of is yourself. If your communication with your teacher is going through a tricky patch, you might ask yourself how you are responding during the lessons. Any change you are in a position to make will be a change in you, so what might that be?

Demonstration

A very useful interactive ploy for the teacher is to demonstrate. When the teacher is playing the student might feel inspired by the brilliance of the teacher's playing, hopefully not overwhelmed by how far out of reach that playing might be for them. The teacher might have to keep in mind that the demonstration is to get a point across rather than impressing the student with their brilliant playing. The essential thing to realize, if you are the student, is that when the teacher plays they are trying to illustrate a point, maybe technical, maybe musical, be clear in your mind what that point is.

Students have to tune into what the message is about and then what the message is. As in all human communication, there is a great capacity for misunderstanding because the receiver has their past experiences as their frame of reference.

Having discussed demonstration with other teachers we know it is not unusual, when demonstrating a bowing technique, to find that the student fixes their eyes on the left hand rather than the bowing. This is often indicative of why the demonstration was necessary in the first place; the student was not aware of how they were using the bow because they were overfocused on the left hand! Telling these students to look at the bowing arm is probably not enough. There needs to be a conversation about how to respond to suggestions and another about awareness and overfocus. We develop the skill of how to direct our attention in a more useful way when we consider the Means-whereby in the perspective of the overall picture.

If a teacher demonstrates the ideal attack on a series of notes, it is only part of the student's job is to observe the musical result. If they then employ their understanding of Use they will soon be able to achieve the result, maybe immediately.

It is very rare that a teacher and their pupil have bodies of identical size, shape and proportions. As the student you have to understand that you and your teacher may well look quite different when you are making the same gestures. The underlying movements will be the same but the superficial impression can be different.

Vivien Mackie, an excellent cellist and Alexander teacher, describes the very good teacher–pupil relationship she had with Pablo Casals. His teaching, as she describes in her book, *Just Play Naturally*[1] can be seen as based on principles very similar to those of Alexander. The book is definitely worth reading.

Heroes

We can look to great players for inspirational models. It may be Roger Federer, if you are interested in Tennis, Fred Astaire, if dancing is your thing or Michael Johnson, if your interest is running. It is very often that you find; whoever is world famous in a chosen field, has excellent Use. Whoever is considered a truly great player of your instrument is worth seeing as well as hearing.

---

[1]Vivien Mackie, *Just Play Naturally*, Xlibris, Bloomington, Indiana, 2006.

In virtually all cases, they will have great Use and because of that, they will make an excellent model.

Student quotes

With the new experience provided by my (cello) teacher, I was sure that I could easily improve my playing but ended up with a back ache and realised what I was doing. I wanted to get a quick result, victim of my End-gaining. I reframed it as, something to work towards, finding a new field of freedom in movement. Therefore I decided to go back to the very first steps. I sat in my chair without the cello and took a moment to listen to my body.

Claire Thirion, cellist

(Working with a challenging young student)

While sitting I worked at opening my back and took care not to fold my arms or legs. I wanted John to feel I was receptive and sympathetic rather than closed off from him. While working at my own Use, I aimed to alter John's by the power of imitation. I found that John responded to my more open and relaxed way of being very quickly, by mirroring my position and matching the speed and volume of my speech. As my improved Use enabled me to be calmer and more positive, John began to develop his potential for calmer emotions.

Elana Eisen, violinist

CHAPTER NINETEEN

Coordination

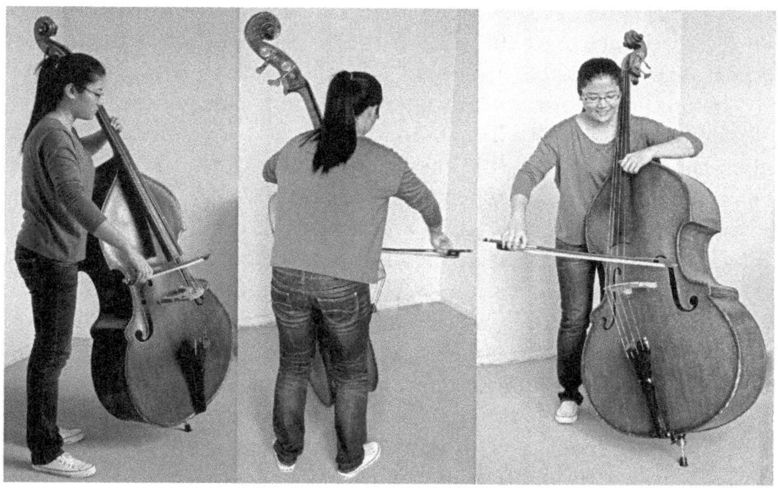

In teaching the principle to a musician the aim is to increase the awareness of himself (or herself) as a whole.[1]

In practice and performance, however, a musician's attention is given almost exclusively to what he is doing with his hands or his feet or his vocal organs, and to the sounds they are producing. Of what he is doing with the

[1]Jones, *Awareness, Freedom and Muscular Control.*

rest of his body, he usually knows very little. In attacking a different problem of technique, the average performer uses two approaches: 'he tries hard' to master it, using all the skill at his command; and if his trying builds up too much tension and fatigues him, he 'relaxes'. In both cases he is working on a trial-and-error basis. He has no way of knowing exactly how much tension is needed, or how to limit it to the time and place where it is wanted.[2]

When we speak we can do it without thinking about technique. We decide what we want to say and out it comes. The ability to use the voice in this way seems to be largely innate. We learnt it when we were younger and the skill is there whenever we want it. We expect it to be possible and it is.

The quality of our voice is also something that we can develop. We need awareness of what we are doing to improve the quality and when the improved quality has been developed, that is a skill that we can ideally draw on whenever we speak. We can be alert to the possibility of losing or not using that developed quality or technique; this is what Alexander developed in his own speaking.

We can develop a similar skill with our musical instrument. There will be thousands of technical issues to address but when we have *really learnt something* it is available for future use without an effort. We want our instrumental technique to function on the level of automatic habit. The risk, when we have worked on an element of technique recently, is that we think about it in performance in the way we thought, to get it to work, in the practice room. That thinking can get in the way of more appropriate thinking for performance. We need to be clear, that this detailed technical thinking is good for the practice room but not the concert platform. When we have learnt something, we have learnt it, we can rely on it if we let our subconscious brain organize it in performance. We want our learnt instrumental technique to work reliably in the background as we rehearse or perform with other musicians. It liberates us to make music.

---

[2]Jones, *Awareness, Freedom and Muscular Control.*

Sensory awareness and the environment

Not having reliable sensory awareness leaves one vulnerable to the vagaries of playing without well-developed technical control. This might work reasonably well most of the time (e.g. in the practice room), but when we have to deal with technical, musical or emotional pressure (e.g. in performance), we can disconnect from the body so our reliability tends to break down.

Being in the Zone

We have probably all had the experience of screwing up a piece of paper and throwing it right across the room and into the middle of the waste paper basket!! We think, 'Wow, that was brilliant and fun, I shall do it again.' When we start thinking about it we focus up and try hard to do it again and we miss the bin. The difference is the first time we let the subconscious organize the weighing of the ball of paper in the hand, the calculation of the distance, the necessary energy to put in the throw and the necessary angle to use so the paper would be falling as it arrived at the opening at the top of the basket. Now we are thinking about it we can see how brilliant the subconscious is at organizing coordination.

We often see the conscious mind messing up the coordination of otherwise elite sportsmen. Golf is a sport where we can see this most clearly. The opponents are not allowed to move your ball or get in the way as you swing the club; in fact they are obliged to stand at a distance in silence as you make your shot.

There are thousands of highly skilled professional golfers playing all over the world. We often see lesser-known players playing brilliant shots and putting themselves in a position to win a big competition. They play at the highest standard until the last few holes; then they start thinking, 'just play these next few holes well and I will win the biggest prize of my life! I must really concentrate on every shot.' When they have those thoughts, they lose the possibility of playing at their highest standard. Their concentration takes them away from the state they were in that facilitated subconscious coordination and they start trying to micro-organize everything they are doing with the conscious brain.

If they had carried on enjoying the experience of playing the game with their highly developed skill in the beautiful environment, sensing the ground under their feet, the breeze on their face, the club in their hands, the shifting weight and flowing energy in their body, they would carry on playing their best game. It is the same for musicians.

- Don't 'try to play well'.
- Enjoy the sense of your body, your instrument and the environment.

We can intelligently develop reliable kinaesthetic and proprioceptive awareness to keep our learnt instrumental technique available. If we become more consciously familiar with that sense of movement, relative position, space within our body and feedback from our contact with the instrument, we tap into a fast and reliable connection with our technique. Our nervous system and subconscious brain work on complex coordination much faster and more reliably than our conscious thought. Interestingly, this all works more reliably if we maintain an awareness of our environment – we can include the environment in our 'expanded field of attention' – our colleagues and the audience are in that environment.

- Include the environment in your expanded field of attention.
- Great musicians are not thinking analytically about their playing in performance.
- Great musicians 'tell the story'.
- Think of David Bowie, Pavarotti, Artur Rubenstein.

Balance and coordination

The body's rebalancing mechanism is an integral part of instrumental coordination. The body rebalances itself within the environment unless we interrupt the mechanism by unbalanced volitional movements or by fixing our body in a position. The concept of 'correct posture' for playing the instrument can be very damaging in this respect. A better idea is to be in a flexible relationship with the instrument that is allowing us to rebalance continuously, including the instrument as part of the total moveable experience. The instrument becomes 'part of us'.

The weight of the instrument and how it moves towards and away from us is something that we can sense as part of our playing. The weight of the instrument connects with our hands and elicits responses from our wrists, arms, shoulders and back; this is very significant; the connection between the hands and the back facilitates coordination with the instrument. Alexander's procedure, 'hands on the back of a chair' (see Chapter 14), helps develop this.

- Include your instrument in your sensory awareness.
- Let your instrument become part of you.

More tension – less sensation

We need to respond to the feedback we get from our sensory nervous system continuously while playing our instrument. The nervous system runs throughout the body; it gives and receives messages to and from our body so we can, when all is working well, move in the way we choose. We need to sense where the various parts of the body are, what state they are in, and how they are moving, so we can play well.

When our volitional muscles are held continuously tense (not what they are designed for), we lose sensation. This does not necessarily stop us from playing but we become less accurate and, of course, we tire sooner. So in that context, we understand that to have the most accurate coordination in any activity we need to use the minimum tension. That way we experience more sensation of what we are doing, we become more alive.

We do, of course need all the necessary, dynamic, physical and emotional movement or right tension! This is very important because the reducing of unnecessary tension should not have the effect of making our performance less energized or less exciting, when those qualities are the essential nature of the music. In fact, distilling our work to 'right tension' makes our performance more energized.

This brings us back to balance. If we are not in balance, the way we stop ourselves falling over is residual tension. Extra tension reduces coordination. If you are in any doubt about this consider this question. If we ask you to thread cotton into a needle, assuming you have good eyesight, you will find it easy enough. Now, if we ask you to hang a bag of shopping on each arm while you thread the needle, will you find the task as easy, even though your hands are available for the needle and cotton? The answer is obviously, 'No!' It will be more difficult because there is tension in muscles over which you need subtle control.

Are you trying hard? (End-gaining)

The habit of trying hard to get a particular result is a frequent source of extra tension. Alexander called this End-gaining. The Alexander approach is to avoid an overriding desire to 'get it right' and consider the Means-whereby – including the Primary Control, awareness of balance and appropriate Direction and then the necessary movements. Keeping an awareness of the environment helps take us away from End-gaining in practice and performance. Think of your favourite player or singer – do they look like they are trying hard?

Timothy Gallwey writes about raising your awareness of what you are doing, rather than the result you are aiming for, in his *Inner Game* books. As Gallwey explains, this allows your subconscious to organize your coordination and that is more accurate and reliable.

- Trying too hard is always counter-productive.

Less tension – more sensation – Direction

So how do we achieve less tension? We should address this as part of our practice. First recognize the excess tension of mind and body as negative habit; this is not always easy. Second, be aware that we want to stop tightening the offending muscles when we go into the activity. Third, we construct Directions that contradict the movement or restriction that the tension is producing.

The strategy more appropriate for the concert hall is simpler – to choose to be aware of the environment. This tends to relieve some of our extra tension. If we become aware of seeing the whole concert hall, we experience more inner freedom and sensation. The same gain comes from listening out into the hall rather than overfocusing on the sound as it leaves our instrument.

Coordination is gained by reflex expansion (in Alexander's terms, lengthening, widening and deepening) or directing our attention to the environment. If you think of lengthening, widening or deepening your body a subtle release tends to happen. By thinking the movements that are the opposite of your habit, your habit is undermined and loses its grip on your movement. It helps to be aware of the space all around you especially above your head and behind your back and that puts you more in touch with the environment.

If we now consider the work from the other end of the chain of reactions, we decide *we want to sense what we are doing, what we are seeing and what we are hearing.* Our desire to prioritize sensory feedback triggers more release in our muscles because we understand, on an innate level, that less tension creates more sensation. Tension is reduced, sensation is increased and we move away from trying hard to play our instrument well to sensing just how we are playing it within the ensemble and the environment.

- Less tension often frees us to be more aware of the environment.
- We create tension in ourselves when we screen out the environment.
- More awareness of the environment frees us up.
- More freedom increases sensory feedback.

Sense the vibrations your instrument

Bring your attention to the vibrations of your instrument being transferred to your body. If you put a hand on your chest and then sing you will feel the vibrations. Put the hand on your head and you will feel the vibrations. Put your hand on a musical instrument while someone is playing it and you will feel the vibrations, in fact as you feel the vibrations your hand will be vibrating as well.

When you are playing or singing your body vibrates less or more according to how much tension you have in your muscles. If you decide you are going to experience this vibration, you will tend to release some of the tension that would otherwise be reducing your sensation. You can have a rich experience of the vibration where you contact your instrument. When this becomes an integral part of playing your coordination will improve.

Space in your body

If you play a large instrument, we have found that you need to create internal space to achieve your best coordination. If you play a small instrument it is just as useful to keep in touch with internal space, in fact all musicians benefit from an awareness of flexible internal space. It is very easy to screen out the sense of space within the body, if the sense of the body goes below the radar. Whatever size you are, think of taking up as much space on Planet Earth as you can, especially when you play your instrument.

Expand your confidence

Another way of seeing this is; to achieve your best coordination you must avoid tightening muscles and that make you smaller. When we expand, we look confident and when we feel confident, we expand! The opposites are also true; when we contract or slump we feel more anxious and when we feel anxious, we contract. Confidence improves coordination – probably the expansion that comes with confidence is the cause of the improvement. We have reflex mechanisms to encourage the body to expand (in Alexander's terms lengthen, widen and deepen), to cope with gravity and air pressure on Planet Earth. Our Direction is used to contradict our negative habits but it is also used to reinvigorate the reflex expansion of the body.

- Occupy your full share of the space on Planet Earth.

Keep your thinking simple in performance

The analytical brain is not good at organizing our coordination directly – it is needed for analysis and the detailed construction or reconstruction of our technique. When we have separated the elements of skill and refined them, we put the elements back together and we use less and less of our analytical brain and leave the coordination of our playing, to the subconscious brain.

You might find it useful to have some key Directions in mind to keep your mind and body working in the most coordinated way, but detailed technical thinking is best in the practice room. We bring our attention to being alive and present with our colleagues and the audience in the concert hall to facilitate our coordination.

Student quotes

Maintaining good Use while developing a technique, for example, playing the violin, enhances our ability to learn. Our responses and reflexes are more accurate due to a more reliable kinaesthetic awareness. Continuing bad body Use results in unbalanced coordination so that some parts of the body do too much work and others do too little.

Kate Robinson, violinist

Keeping the thought of an upward Direction acting upon my head at the forefront of my mind, I could not believe the difference this made to my playing. I finally felt that I had experienced the fact that practising Alexander Technique dramatically improves coordination, as my performance was much more accurate than any time that I had practiced it.

Catherine Hare, flautist

CHAPTER TWENTY

Instrumental technique

Talent may be expressed as a capacity for coordination. It is my contention that to increase one's capacity for coordination, however slightly is infinitely more rewarding than any amount of hard labour at the keyboard which does not serve that purpose.[1]

Harold Taylor

Drumming

---

[1]Harold Taylor, *The Pianist's Talent*, Long Beach, 1987, p.

The big message here is: The way you use your mind and body *is the way that you play your instrument.* It is not just that 'it has an influence on the way you play your instrument.' So it is, in our opinion, vital to understand that, *your instrumental technique is the way you use your mind and body.*

The Alexander Technique is continuously looking at the way you use your mind and body. Part of playing your instrument will be standing or sitting. If, as you read this book, you are consciously working on improving your standing or sitting it will have an influence on how you stand or sit now and how you stand or sit in the future. It will, of course, influence what you get from reading this book now, and it will influence your playing when you go to your instrument. The same can be said of how you are using your eyes and how you are breathing.

- Your instrumental technique is *the way you use your mind and body!*
- Consciously consider your standing and sitting, it will improve your instrumental technique.

Loss of good Use

Let us consider how an old person might become stooped, bent almost double over their walking stick. Is it inevitable that old people will be that sort of shape? Well the answer has to be no! If you look at photographs of Artur Rubenstein in his eighties and nineties he was open and upright. His Use had been good throughout his earlier life, that is how he played so well in his early and middle life and we know he continued to play brilliantly to the end of his life. It is not a surprise, considering his Use, that he was re-recording the Beethoven sonatas when he was 90.

The stooped old person gets into that shape in the same way a stooped young person does. They lose the in-built reflex response to gravity that is programmed into us all to keep us lengthening and widening with a free rebalancing head on the top of the body. To reiterate the point that is too important to make once, this rebalancing state is not posture that we can choose when we need it; it is a state of mind and body that we are designed to be in continuously. If we have lost it from our lives we can restore it by 'Constructive Conscious Control' – applying the Alexander principles.

- If you have lost the reflex-facilitated support in your body, you can restore it.

Send your head up!

Whatever we are doing we can send the head up to recover lengthening and balance. Whatever we are playing benefits from the same upward thinking. When the playing needs to be soft, some players tend to make themselves smaller; that makes it more difficult to control the instrument. When you need to play louder any extra tension necessary should be used but ask yourself, 'is extra tension necessary and if so, can I do less than I am?'

- If you need to play louder think your head up!
- If you need to play softer, think your head up!
- If you are a wind or brass player encourage your spine to lengthen on the out-breath.
- In some players there is a tendency to pull or squeeze down towards the end of the out-breath; it might give you a sense of more power when you collapse the upper body and squeeze air out in this way but this contradiction of the human design will tend to bring a loss of coordination and the naturally occurring *ideal* 'support' of the sound will be reduced.
- The feeling of more control or security, from extra tension, can be an illusion and Alexander found this often to be the case.
- Direct yourself into the space above, behind and around you.

Connect your hands with your back

The instrumental technique for every musical instrument includes a connection with your back. Your breathing will improve if your back is doing the job for which it is designed. Your arms can get a lot of help from a well organized back. Your arm movements and your hand movements will be more fluent and precise if your back helps support them. There are various Alexander practices that help develop this connection: 'Hands on the Back of a Chair' (Chapter 14); 'Semi-supine' and 'Semi-supine Plus' (Chapter 13); 'Hands on the Wall', 'Back on the Wall' and 'Crawling' (Chapter 16).

Lead your arms with your hands

We have discussed how the head leads and the body follows. It is also the case that the hands lead and the arms follow. Whatever your instrument, if you take your hands to where they need to be, your arms will tend to have done just what is necessary. This is quite different to putting your arms in the correct position with your hands on the ends of them. This is a valuable idea when bowing a string instrument. Send your head up and your hand away from your back to establish good bow contact with the string. The left hand leads the arm into any necessary movement; this approach avoids lifting your elbow into less coordinated attempts to get it in the right position.

- The head leads, the body follows.
- The hands lead, the arms follow.

How to turn to your instrument

Some instruments are awkward to get a human body around to play. Some need a certain amount of turn in the body to set up the playing relationships necessary; the flute is a prime example. A good rule of thumb is, if a turn is necessary, spread it over more of the body rather than a more extreme torque over less of the body. Thinking of an example; a double bass has a large box; most players need to twist anticlockwise to bow on the top string, if the player is standing, the whole body can be involved in the turn so no localized part has a lot of work to do.

- Include your whole body in turning to play your instrument.

Depressing the keys, valves or strings

When it comes to pressing the keys, valves or the strings down on the instrument, sensory feedback is again vitally important. There is always some sort of response from the key, valve or the string as they are designed to spring back. To overpower the springy resistance is not usually hard work; we should seriously consider if there is any advantage in pressing harder than necessary when making the movement.

If there is an advantage, for example, making a clearer sound on a string instrument, we have to weigh in the balance the loss of facility that comes with that extra tension in the muscles involved. It is useful to sense the springy resistance of the instrument's mechanism and, as much as possible, feel the instrument pushing the fingers away after they have done their job. Tuning into that feeling will tend to reduce unnecessary tension and improve facility and coordination.

- Sense your instrument pushing your fingers away.

Accents

Accents can disturb coordination. If your head gets involved with making the accent the Primary Control suffers. The player may well feel they have made a strong accent but was it a strong accent? Was there a loss of control because of the compromise to the head–neck–back relationship? So, consider your Primary Control and make use of your technical knowledge of how to make an accent on your instrument.

How the great players play

Your instrumental technique will obviously depend on what you play but in our experience of teaching the Alexander Technique to musicians, there are virtually no contradictions between

Alexander's principles and the received wisdom handed down in the treatises of the various instruments over the centuries. When we pursue any apparent contradictions with living instrumental teachers it usually only takes a brief conversation to find that we agree but we were using words slightly differently.

As musicians share ideas and refine their mutually agreed 'best practice', instrumental technique that acknowledges the design of the human body becomes the accepted wisdom for each instrument. Very talented musicians with the best Use, rise to the top of the tree. These musicians are then encouraged to write the treatises and the advice tends to be good. This points to the fact that however talented you are, an understanding of 'good Use' will facilitate the reliable development of good instrumental technique and help you reach your full potential as a musician.

Read the treatises with Alexander in mind

It is good practice to read any treatise written on the playing of your instrument by an accepted authority. Bring your knowledge of 'good Use' to your appreciation of the advice and you will make the time spent reading the treatise even more valuable. Sometimes, the advice is about the results you should be looking for or what you should do, without an explanation of how to do it. You will then have to experiment.

The Alexander principles can be used to guide your practice in the search for 'how to do it'.

The same applies if you are starting, more or less, from scratch, for example, trying to discover a certain type of articulation, without advice from a teacher. If you are balancing with the instrument, starting with the head being free on the top of the spine and an expanding tendency throughout your body, you will often find solutions easily and efficiently. It is when we try hard and 'strain every sinew to make it happen' that we struggle to make progress.

Experiment and get it wrong

If you look after your Use and experiment with your new technical ideas or the new ideas from your teacher, you will not go far wrong. Getting it wrong is a big part of practice and the learning process. A healthy attitude to making 'mistakes' or getting things 'wrong' opens up the possibility of stress-free progress. If you are desperate to get everything right all the time, the pressure builds up and stops you experimenting freely in your practice.

Body map your instrumental technique

When considering instrumental technique it is very useful to 'body map' the moving parts. To get a sound out of any musical instrument you need to move your body. We are designed to move at joints. What joints are involved in playing your instrument? When you have a clear *and accurate* perception of where your body is and how it is designed to move, your movements will be fluent and your coordination reliable, for example, the way your arms move depends on your deep-seated perception of where all your joints are.

For all instruments you need a clear map of your arms. Mapping the shoulder connection at the collarbone's joint with the sternum (breast bone) is critical for fluent, back supported, arm movement. Mapping how the forearm bones move when you play is very influential. If you know that your hand joins onto one of the two bones in the forearm (the radius, on the thumb side), that will improve your instrumental technique. For many instruments, mapping the anatomy of the hand (wrist bones and fingers) can increase your facility.

If you plan to breathe while you are playing, and you probably realize that is essential whatever your instrument, Body Mapping the joints at both ends of the ribs helps free up your breathing.

If you think that you do not use your legs when you play your instrument, think again. Whether you are standing or sitting, your legs will contribute to your upper body support. Clear ideas of where your hip joints and sitting bones are, and where your knees, ankles and feet are, will improve your chances of playing with your whole body as a coordinated unit. (See Chapter 9 for more detail about Body Mapping.)

Particular instrumental issues

Every musician will have their own unique way of using their mind and body when they play. It is very helpful to have individual

Alexander lessons to receive advice about your unique patterns of Use.

In our experience at the RCM, we have noticed certain trends that seem to come up for certain instruments. These trends are, of course, not universal, but it is worth casting an eye on our observations of what tends to come up with your instrument, to see if you share the pattern of Use.

We are not suggesting that we know how to play all instruments but we have had great success in helping students of all instruments by looking at their patterns of Use with our 'Alexander eyes' and suggesting how to apply the Alexander principles to the art and craft of playing. When we identify negative patterns involved in playing or simply holding the instrument, we can help those players recognize the problem and give them tools to change.

Violin and viola

The classic pattern is to raise the left shoulder, tighten the jaw and pull the head down onto the chin rest. The head is not always free on the top of the spine. The weight is often more on the left than the right foot and the pelvis is often held forward. The left elbow is often tightened and pushed further than necessary under the instrument. The eyes often stare at the left hand when playing without music.

Cello

Cellists often lean back at the hip joints then wrap their thorax round the body of the instrument with the head held forwards in space over the instrument. The head is then often pulled back and down in relation to the spine (Alexander's original habit); this tendency is usually exaggerated when playing in high positions. Almost all cellists have their head displaced to the right, away from the instrument, to take their neck clear of the 'C' string peg. The left shoulder is often raised. The weight is often more on the right sitting bone than the left. The thumbs often lack freedom.

Double bass

Bass players have similar patterns to cellists (mentioned earlier) when sitting to play. When standing, the player's weight is often moved more onto the right foot. The left shoulder is usually raised and pulled back – the right shoulder pulled down. Sitting bass players often arch the low back in low positions. The right thumb is often tight and overstraightened (or even bent back) on the bow.

Oboe, clarinet, recorder (and similar)

When standing the pelvis is often thrown forward of the ankles and atlanto-occipital joint, narrowing the back and restricting the breathing. Sometimes the head is pulled back (in relation to the spine) and the vocal folds partially closed (making an audible noise) when the player is breathing in. The head is often taken forward in space to the instrument and the jaw held with excess tension. Many times we see shoulders raised and pulled forward. The legs are frequently braced when standing and the hips restricted when sitting. Accents can include pulling the head down.

Flute

The almost universal pattern is to position the instrument lower than horizontal and compensate by bending the neck to the right to get the head and so the mouth arriving at the lip-plate at the most efficient angle for tone production. This sets a scoliosis (a sideways bend in the spine) in place and restricts the breathing. The lack of resistance from the instrument (inherent in the flute) when blowing seems to make the tendency for the head to be moved forward to the instrument more pronounced. Some flautists pull their right shoulder back, weakening the connection between the hands and the back. Some raise and push the left shoulder forward. Ideally there is a turning movement of the complete upper body when sitting, or the whole body when standing, keeping the shoulders well connected to the back. The weight is often more on the right sitting bone when sitting or the right foot when standing. The wrists are often put under stress by holding the elbows too far away from each other.

Bassoon

The bassoon is a heavy instrument. If a neck strap is used it is a real challenge to avoid the head being pulled forward and down in space, then the head is pulled back in relation to the spine to meet the reed. A well-adjusted body harness can apparently reduce the challenge. The seat strap seems to be a popular option; it is important, with a seat strap, to be aware of forward movement being at the hip joints. Sometimes the pelvis remains static on the chair to keep the strap clamped on the chair. Sitting using a spike can take a good deal of the weight away from the body but the spike must be long enough to deliver the reed to the mouth without having to pull the head forward or down in space. The fitting of the equipment to the player seems absolutely vital; the spike and the crook should be fitted when the player's Use is as good as possible. The right shoulder of many bassoonists is pulled back, disconnecting the hand and arm from the back's support. The weight of the instrument being on the hands of the player will affect the facility and coordination of the bassoonist, so any arrangement to reduce that weight is positive.

Brass players

All brass players tend to **reach** for the mouthpiece by moving their head forward in space whereas bringing the instrument to the mouth is ideal. Learning to sit or stand in a balancing state, with the instrument included in the balance, is a good start to sorting out this problem.

Trumpet

The big tendency when standing is to throw the pelvis forward and brace the legs under the instrument, then fix the arms in position, both patterns restrict the breathing. Quite often trumpeters stiffen their fingers on the valves.

Trombone

Players often move their head forward to meet the mouthpiece. The left hand and arm become fixed in position. The head, right arm and shoulder are pulled down as the slide is taken forward. There is often a lack of freedom in the right shoulder that restricts free movement of the slide.

Horn

This is another heavy instrument. Players often pull the right shoulder back, losing connection with and support from the back muscles. This also narrows the back, which restricts the breathing. The head is sometimes pulled back on the in-breath. It is good to look out for raising the chest on in-breaths. Some players have a support under their instrument, resting on their right leg, which reduces the burden of the instrument's weight on the upper body.

Tuba

Tuba players vary quite a lot but many large players pull themselves down onto the instrument. The instrument is best supported by the chair, your legs or a stand, with any packing necessary to bring the mouthpiece to your mouth. The problem of the weight of the instrument can be minimized by keeping your upper body lengthening and perpendicular. The instrument can be fitted to the player by having the lead tube to the mouthpiece adjusted to have the instrument as perpendicular as the upper body.

Harp

Players tend to lean back from the hips and then the head comes forward over the instrument, similar to cellists. The legs are often rather tense with restricted movement in the hips, knees and ankles. The hand shapes are often held in tension when the fingers could be releasing. There is a tendency for the right shoulder to be pulled back, losing connection with the back's natural support. A spiral turn of the whole body, when necessary, is more conducive to comfort and coordination.

Piano

Many pianists pull their head towards the keyboard. The leg joints lack freedom and many do not really balance on their sitting bones. The hands often carry more than the necessary tension. Holding the elbows in uncoordinated positions can restrict movement of the lower arms. We look for the hands to be orientated inside the little fingers rather than outside the thumbs; this improves the use of the forearms and so the coordination.

Organ

Organists have a challenge in not being able to put their feet down, so the legs cannot share the work of supporting the upper body, except briefly when playing each pedal note. They often end up leaning back at the hips to take the weight off their feet and then pulling the head down, inverting the lumbar and cervical curves and exaggerating the thoracic curve. The legs need to be free at all the joints and the whole body has to perform challenging balancing acts that constantly change according to what is being played with hands and feet. Organists, like other humans, have better coordination when the spine is lengthening and the back widening.

Guitar

The guitar is played in many different ways: hung round the neck; propped on the leg, directly or with an attachment, foot up/foot down. Having a foot on a footstool tends to throw the weight onto the right sitting bone but it is possible to keep the weight more or less balancing over the two sitting bones if you find the necessary freedom in the hip joints. Guitarists tend to stare at their left hand; the eyes can be less focused to great effect. The upper body often wraps round the body of the instrument.

Singers

Singers often raise the chest, tightening the lumbar muscles and restricting some ideal breathing movements. They are sometimes not grounded, often with their weight thrown forward towards the audience. They might pull the head back to open the mouth and partially close the vocal folds on the in-breath. They often overfocus their eyes on a point at the back of the hall.

Elizabeth Langford looks in detail about some specific issues for musicians in her book (*Mind Muscle and Music*). There are chapters for the common instruments, voice and conductors.[2]

A large part of our work with the students at the RCM is to observe their Use. If a student is not balanced we help them bring their attention to this vital part of their playing technique. If we see that a musician is restricting their movements in any way, we help them to construct suitable Directions to use on a daily basis to reverse any negative patterns. The work becomes more refined as the habits weaken and when the patterns have gone we can work on a different area of the musician's Use.

We are convinced that it is possible to play all musical instruments in balance and to recover balance if it is lost. It is possible for all players to be comfortable. We notice that when a musician uses all the necessary changing tensions and no extra tensions, their playing tends to be well coordinated and they are always comfortable. Students with an accurate 'body map' move more efficiently than those without. Students with effortless technique can express themselves fluently. Musicians who have excellent Use are usually capable of performing well, even when they feel under pressure their instrumental technique is reliable.

Student quotes

Lengthen, widen, broaden . . . are the keywords. When I practise I tend to shrink, i.e. to close the space around my

[2]Elizabeth Langford, *Mind and Muscle and Music*, Alexandertechniek Centrum vzw, Leuven, 2008.

violin by closing up the arms and bending down my head. That impairs everything: my primary control is affected, the sound closes down, and my whole attitude becomes low in energy and introvert. Whereas I should: free the neck, widen the back, lengthen the spine, and so my throat and plexus will be free – and so my breathing will expand! I wrote down the principles above and put them in my violin case so they are always at hand.

Anne-Catherine Berrut, violinist

When the head is balanced on top of the spine with the oboe in a natural position the pitch is more consistent throughout the instrument and it was simply easier to blow into. The sound is also more resonant and richer. This is true for articulation as well – if the head is pulled and pushed into awkward positions the oral cavity changes shape and the passageway from the throat to the mouth becomes restricted, inhibiting the tongue from articulating correctly, particularly in faster passages.

Rebecca Cass, oboist

CHAPTER TWENTY-ONE

What is good practice?

If you stop doing the wrong thing, the right thing will do itself.

F. M. Alexander

Felicity in balance, ready for good practice

Practice is one of the challenges of learning a musical instrument. There are a few qualities that we can almost certainly agree on.

- It should be efficient (whatever that means to us).
- It should improve something.
- We should be aware of what we have changed for future use.
- We should be physically comfortable during and after the practice.
- We should feel good about what we have done.

The following are other extremely beneficial qualities that come as part of an 'Alexander' approach to practice:

- A clear structure with a balance between playing and analysis, maybe using semi-supine (see Chapter 13) when analysing and planning.
- A psychophysical awareness throughout the practice.
- A continuous rebalancing of the primary control (see Chapter 5) and the body as a whole.
- A clear and accurate 'body map' (see Chapter 9) when playing.
- Efficient, free breathing (see Chapter 10).
- Good Use of the visual mechanism (see Chapter 12).
- Awareness of the balance between attention to detail and keeping an overview of the big picture.
- Awareness that you can choose to be present.

How long should we practise?

If you want to become an excellent musician you will need to practise for thousands of hours. But it is a good idea not to do too many of them in one session.

As an intelligent human being you can practise very efficiently for a certain period. I would like to share part of my musical story with you; it demonstrates that I did not use all of my intelligence when I was in my late teens and early twenties.

How many hours? (Peter's story)

I used to clock up the hours and feel very good about myself. I would tell my friends, with pride, that I had practised for hours and lost all sense of the time. I realize my hour count was never challenged by the question, 'and what did you learn or achieve?' I managed to practise my double bass until I ached all over, my fingers bled and my vision became unreliable. I felt very committed to this macho practice style until my body screamed at me to stop! In fact it did stop and I had to recover in bed until the pain reduced enough to get out of bed and inflict more punishment on my mind and body.

20 minutes brilliant playing

With the insight that I gained through studying the Alexander Technique I have changed my pattern of practice dramatically. I have experimented with how much playing practice is possible at my absolute best level and found that 20 minutes is about the limit. After that it becomes good practice, no longer brilliant. So I stop playing after 20 minutes but I continue practising by lying in semi-supine position for about 10 minutes. I review how my playing practice went during the last 20 minutes. I give myself some time experiencing the full effect of gravity and give myself some Alexandrian Direction. I make a detailed plan of what I am going to achieve during my next 20 minutes of playing. I have very clear intentions, whether that is changing instrumental technique, memorizing a passage, characterizing a section of orchestral or solo repertoire – whatever I need to work on next. I am happy to keep the changes simple, for greater clarity. I am also keen to reassess the big picture. I ask myself constructive questions to reassess my intentions: What am I trying to achieve? When is the next concert? Where is the weakness in my technique/interpretation? Am I enjoying myself as much as possible?

Structure your practice

The practice structure set out in the previous paragraph is suggested to all students at the RCM, during their first-year introductory Alexander course. We have received extremely positive feedback from countless students. Some students have not been able to bring themselves to try the idea because they are not prepared to stop playing when they have 'practice time'. Some of those students reappear a year or two later, asking for some Alexander lessons with the intention of getting out of pain. They then try the idea and find it is part of their pain solution. They are also amazed that with less playing during practice time, they make more progress!

Are there exceptions?

A few musicians, with exceptional Use, might be able to practise intensely and brilliantly for 30 minutes and then take 5 minutes break from playing but they are exceptional. Thousands of hours of inefficient, damaging work are going on in practice rooms at conservatories all over the world. Those hours could be transformed into productive practice, simply by changing the basic structure and including 'semi-supine'.

Are you dehydrated?

We all know that we need to keep topping up our water level. Humans have a lot of water in the body. We need about two and a half litres of water from drinks and food every day. The brain needs plenty of water to keep sending and receiving the electronic messages to and from the central nervous system. It is a good habit to take water to your practice room and then keep drinking a little regularly throughout your practice session.

Keep breathing

If there is a window in your practice room, open it! Oxygen is food for the brain, it keeps you alert and productive; a stuffy room makes good practice virtually impossible. To practise or perform well we need to breathe well. We notice that musicians who do not breathe freely seem to struggle with their awareness of tempo, so if consistency of tempo is an issue for you, monitor your breathing. String players who hold their breath often have trouble shifting; sometimes they suspend the breath just before big shifts (holding the breath is often an expression of anxiety or doubt). We need to consciously monitor our (usually subconscious) reflex breathing; to notice if it is flowing easily when we are focusing on details or playing complex, demanding passages; you can record yourself so you are more likely to notice if your breathing is disturbed. If you look in a mirror when you are playing and see your face tensing up near the eyes, nose or mouth, you are probably losing freedom in your breathing. Muscles stop working accurately when starved of oxygen.

If we stop practising and have a short walk, we can often notice the effect of getting more oxygen in the blood. If this improves the situation it suggests that you are not breathing freely enough to maintain the alertness that will facilitate brilliant practice and help you enjoy the work. (See Chapter 10: Breathing, for more details.)

- Take an occasional short walk during practice sessions.
- Monitor your breathing.

Include your eyes

Great musicians have flexible eyes that see their colleagues, their music and the audience. Overfocusing cuts down your awareness of some useful cues but it also compromises your coordination. When you are practising music that you don't know very well it is easy to stare at the music as if latching on to the page with extreme focus gives you a better chance of playing it well. In fact, locking onto the music with your eyes seems to reduce your chances, even when you are sight-reading. We find that students at the RCM who are not glued to the music are usually more fluent readers and players. The way forward is to practise with your vision in mind and notice how quickly you absorb the information on the page.

> After being aware of my vision and remaining in 'panoramic', whilst performing tasks at the piano, I noticed a clear change in the speed that I was able to learn repertoire.
>
> Nick Mccarthy, pianist

When you have practised enough to feel confident to free up the use of your eyes in a practice situation, you may feel the stakes are too high to do the same in concerts. That is a return of the old fear. A very important breakthrough occurs when you 'let go' of the score in concerts – *remember your coordination is at stake.* (For more detail on vision, see Chapter 12.)

- Let go of any fear around losing your place in the music.

Mental chatter

Do you sometimes find your mind has wandered? It is good to notice if you have a voice in your head running a commentary on your practice trying to encourage you to take your attention elsewhere. The voice in the head is often making negative remarks, 'you messed that up yesterday', 'that was just not good enough', 'this is the sort of bit you don't play well.' This sort of commentary has a negative effect on your emotional state. You might try to ignore it but find that the effort to ignore it leaves you feeling agitated rather than calm and confident with relaxed concentration.

If you notice a voice in your head, try accepting it as a habit that will sabotage your practice. A way of dealing with your mental chatter is to see it as 'unfinished business' to be dealt with at a later date, for now bring your thoughts back to the present. Some people like to see these thoughts like a passing bus; you don't have to jump on. The basic message is to choose to be truly present with what you are doing, now!

- Bring your attention to what is happening now.

Remember to remember

A good practice tip to bring yourself back to sensory awareness is to add small red dots to your music. As you arrive at a dot it reminds you to expand your field of attention, to look out, breathe and balance. These memory joggers will help by reminding you to 'be in the Zone'. They can even stay with you when you have memorized the piece.

Some specific applications of the technique to practice

To change the way you hold your instrument

Let us say you have decided that you will hold the instrument at a different angle. It is very easy to get focused on the suggestion that you have received from your teacher or a colleague and see the change of hand or arm position or the angle of the instrument to you as the whole change. From an Alexander perspective, you would consider the big picture; you would consider the quality of your Primary Control and your overall balance (including the instrument). You could 'body map' the joints involved in holding the instrument, so you are likely to move freely where you are making the changes. You can bring your attention to your sense of where your body is and what it is doing, bearing in mind that your sense of the position and movement of your body might be misleading (Faulty Sensory Perception). You can check, by looking in a mirror, that you are in fact doing what you think you are doing. You might notice if your idea of the new arrangement with the instrument is a static position rather than a state of rebalancing with your instrument.

It is useful to notice your emotional reaction to the idea of this change and whether you are trying to get the change done as soon as possible or just engaging in the process without putting pressure on yourself to succeed as soon as possible. You may well reconsider why you are making this change and what you are sensing as you work on it.

Inhibition

Your relationship with the instrument will have been developed and ingrained over months or years; it will tend to be habitual and usually subconscious. Your habit will be tending to organize how you take the instrument in your hands even when you are intending it to do it differently. Your habit will also be influencing your perception of any changes you are making; you will feel the new pattern in relation to the old. The old familiar feeling will be a strong element of your old way of holding the instrument; it might have a feeling of 'right' about it, even though you have decided to change it. You can facilitate the change to the new way by consciously expecting and intending to feel different. You can speed up the change to the new technique by having a clear intention to stop holding the instrument in the old way: this is an example of Inhibition. This idea is different from simply planning to hold the instrument differently; the Inhibition wipes the slate clean before you work on the new plan.

Means-whereby

> *You cannot solve a problem from the same consciousness that created it. You must learn to see the world anew.*
>
> Albert Einstein

If your work is going well you will be full of curiosity to experience holding and playing your instrument in the new way with no fixed expectation. You can reassess how the change is going by asking constructive questions:

- Can I replace my ambition with curiosity?
- Why am I making this change?
- Am I staying with the plan?
- Am I in balance?
- Am I breathing and can I see the room around me?

A curiosity to sense the potential of the new way is vital. The thought, 'this feels strange or wrong' might well be there because you are sensing that you are doing something different from the old pattern. You can see the 'strange feeling' as positive because it means you are changing something. As you become used to working in this way you may well find, more often than not, that you embrace change with a feeling that you enjoy freshness and find the new sensations interesting.

If you are free to rebalance, any localized change will affect the whole body; it is important that we keep allowing small local adjustments to have knock-on effects throughout the whole body so the change is integrated through the reflex rebalancing mechanisms that optimize our coordination.

As we play hour after hour, we create an extended body map (see Chapter 9) that includes the instrument. We become aware of its movement as if it were part of our body. This starts with our contact with the instrument but we can develop sensitivity to how it is vibrating while we are playing. The patterns of movement of our musical instrument are included in our neural perceptions, whether that is the movement of a bow, the travel of a valve or key or the vibrating of the reed or the body of the instrument. This 'tuning in' to the position, movement and vibration of our instrument is working best for us all the time we have the minimum tension or stress in our mind and body. Light directed movements with minimum tension for the activity are what we are looking for.

Repetition

> *Repetition is the mother of skill so long as there's skill in the repetition.*[1]

Mindless repetition is counter-productive and is best avoided. Repetition is, however, an important device. When we repeat an action or a passage of music we make recall on future occasions more fluent. The skill moves more into the automatic, subconscious

---

[1]Paul Chek, Scientific Back Training Correspondence Course, Vista CA 1993.

realm making it faster and more efficient. The danger is the deeper it goes the less changeable it can become. As musicians we need to feel confident that we can play our part in an ensemble situation but have the flexibility to change what we have learnt in an instant, often subtly but sometimes dramatically. If we repeat elements of technique or music in our practice with an expanding sense of the possible variations in our mind and body, we will build in flexibility. In some languages the word for 'repetition' is used for 'rehearsal'. 'Rehearing' something also implies repetition, but there is a suggestion of possible reassessment.

Practise without the instrument

It can be very useful to practise away from your instrument. You can obviously make use of travelling time for practising in your imagination. Including the Alexander connections that you make in your lessons or find in this book makes that 'mental practice' more effective. Journeys are particularly good for thinking through playing whole pieces or whole programmes, especially if you are going to play from memory. If you can successfully imagine playing through a piece without a score, you are ready to play it from memory. Imagining actually playing through music on your instrument will activate the muscles that actually shorten and lengthen when you play for real. It is good to sense the movements in you and your instrument as you think through the piece; make it as vivid a sensory experience as you can by bringing your attention to the changing sensations as you imagine playing. If it is a programme for an upcoming concert, imagine the venue, your colleagues and the audience as vividly as possible as well as your playing.

If you are in a practice session and you are struggling with a particular section you might choose to stop playing and imagine playing the passage successfully. By thinking through the section you will create a mental clarity that will improve your coordination. Exactly the same thinking that is used for your imaginary playing is necessary for the real thing; the advantage is that you do not have the distracting stimulus of actually playing the instrument while trying to sort out your thinking. If you cannot think through the passage and imagine yourself playing it easily, you have little chance of playing it. We can get drawn into playing the passage again and again until we get through it; however, if the mental clarity is what is missing, and it often is, mental practice can be the Means-whereby you take the next step towards finding the solution.

Find a 'Practice Partner'

It is very powerful to practise with a friend present, a 'Practice Partner'. You can develop a reciprocal arrangement and find how best to support each other. It makes concentration easier as there is a sense of responsibility to the friend who is sharing their time with you. Being interactive is usually very helpful for most human activities but it is obviously a strong part of ensemble playing. You can share your intentions with your practice friend. You know they will notice whether you are sticking to your intentions, making it more likely that you shall. The problem of Faulty Sensory Awareness, which is responsible for so many negative patterns, can be tackled using the independent observations from your friend. It does not have to be a long session for this to be useful. Asking constructive questions when you have been listening is often more productive than giving direct advice, for example, 'could you sense what was happening in your breathing when you played the high passage?' The answering of the questions will help to increase awareness, refine and improve the accuracy of sensing of what you are doing. There is no better atmosphere in a shared practice session than non-judgemental support, with a certain amount of humour thrown in, if possible.

Using a video camera

It is very useful to set up a video camera to record your practice. You are carrying on practising when you are listening to the recording and watching what you were doing. You can become your own teacher. Often musicians are surprised that some passages they thought were not well played were actually very effective. Conversely, some passages that felt and even sounded good at the time were unclear, out of tune or not rhythmic. Many of us have access to video cameras; some of us even have them on our mobile phones. They are a great resource when it comes to practice; unlike a mirror; we see the image the correct way round. We can replay passages hearing and seeing what we were doing; this allows us to be more objective. When we play again the experience of seeing as well as hearing what we did will inform how we play next, both consciously and to a certain extent subconsciously. A double bass playing friend of ours said he liked to play as little as possible to keep his fingers sensitive; he videoed all his practice and watched it several times before playing again. His results were excellent. The way you use your body is there on the screen and you will hear that Use Affects Functioning!

Feel what it sounds like!

If you are listening while you are playing, it is useful to get in touch with your other sensory feedback: touch, sense of weight, pressure, balance and movement; they can be very informative. 'When my playing sounds like this, my body feels like this!' The feeling is more immediate than the sound. You can get a sense of what you are doing and how you will play before and during the creation of sound. If you are waiting to hear the sound, it is too late to change what you have played. To make this point specifically, if you play a short note and listen for if it is tune or not, you are too late. If you develop your sensory feedback of what you are doing and the way the instrument is responding as you touch or move it, you have a better chance of the note you are about to play starting in tune. The same can be said for attack, resonance, and so on. So a lively interest in accurate sensory perception, especially the kinaesthetic sense is a quality of good practice.

Mind and body work as one

This brings us back to Alexander's idea of Psychophysical Unity. The mind and body are divisible by an analytical human for convenience when thinking and discussing the human condition, but in living they work as an indivisible unit. The French Revolution confirmed that without the head well attached to the rest of the body, both the head and the rest of the body stop working. If your mind and body are functioning perfectly the central nervous system will be receiving and giving accurately perceived messages from one to the other. If your mind and body are not functioning optimally, probably the normal state of affairs for most humans, applying Alexander's principles will continuously improve your performance. We are designed to expand and balance and our playing will improve easily if we do. Using Direction can stimulate the tendency to expand and balance the body. If we include an expansion of the mind and body in practice situations, we usually enjoy ourselves and it will tend to be 'good practice'.

For example, if your head is not being allowed to rebalance itself many times a second, you may be trying very hard but failing to get a result. The result will be achieved more easily if you attend to the restoration of the balance of your Primary Control. If you spend more time trying to get the result by repetition with more and more effort it will take you much longer. Looking at your approach to problem solving in practice is fundamental to 'good practice'.

Keep a practice diary

Many of our students have found it useful to keep an Alexander practice diary. If you write down what you plan to achieve in your next practice or what you managed to work on during your last practice it helps maintain the vitality and integrity of your work.

Summary

- Do plenty of conscious practice.
- Plan and structure your practice.
- Work at being comfortable.
- Include awareness of your Primary Control – remember the French Revolution.
- Include reflex rebalancing of your whole body.
- Don't play for too long.
- Use 'semi-supine', 'review' and 'detailed planning'.

- Remember that Use affects functioning.
- Be aware of what you are doing while you are doing it.
- Be aware that your feelings can mislead you.
- Use a mirror – video camera – a friend.
- Breathe freely.
- Use your vision well.
- Use your imagination – practise without the instrument.
- Maintain awareness of the big picture when attending to details.
- Feel what it sounds like.
- If you are not comfortable it is not good practice.
- Have fun!

Student quotes

For many years I believed that pain after practising was a normal consequence of good work. By taking Alexander lessons I learned to be more aware of misuse. As a result, instead of playing in a way that develops repetitive practice with bad habits, I decided to make the choice to get rid of all the unnecessary stiffness which does not help to solve the real problems. In this way I made it clear to myself that without Inhibition I will just go on repeating my mistakes.

Claire Thirion, cellist

I was delighted with the philosophy of letting change happen and for once not 'having to be good' at something.

Miranda Barritt, cellist

PART SIX
Performance

CHAPTER TWENTY-TWO

Performance anxiety

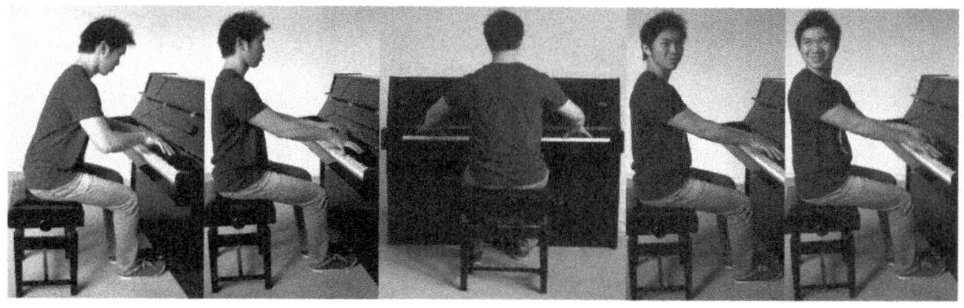

Your emotional condition is far more influential on your performance than hours and hours of practice. There are musicians – some say there were more of them in the past – who get as much pleasure from a performance as they give, who always perform easily and well, and who use themselves so efficiently that their professional lives and their natural lives coincide. There are others, however, with equal talent and training, to whom performance and even practice are exhausting, and whose professional lives are cut short because they lose the mastery of the skills they have acquired. They put forth more effort in solving technical problems than the results warrant, and ultimately discover that they

have used up their reserves of energy. If they understood the use of themselves as well as they understood the use of their instruments, such breakdowns would be far less frequent.

F. P. Jones[1]

The way Alexander saw things: our emotional condition is expressed throughout the whole human organism, the mind and body, the complete Psychophysical Self.

What are the fears involved?

We all have our own particular mixture of fears. There are different types of fear, for example:

- Fear of failure because we would lose face.
- Fear of not being as good as other musicians.
- Fear of having a memory lapse.

The list could go on for a long time. Any one or a mixture of fears can impair your ability to play your instrument beautifully, to play your part accurately and/or to communicate with your colleagues and the audience. This could be described as 'underperforming'.

We need to accept that our reaction to the situation is manifested in our emotional state, throughout our whole being. We tighten our muscles, interfere with our breathing, balance and vision, and that is just for starters. It is not the external circumstances, for example, the concert, the concerto or the audition that is the problem. It is useful to accept that we are creating the state that we are in, so, if we are anxious or nervous and it is having a negative affect on our performance, 'we are messing ourselves up!'

You cannot tell yourself what to feel but you can put constructive thinking in place. Some people find it possible to reframe their thinking and see the nervous energy as extra performance energy.

---

[1]Jones, *Awareness, Freedom and Muscular Control.*

So when nervous energy arrives in you, you can experiment with redirecting it, as extra potential, into your performance. Using the Alexander Technique, we are choosing to put in place the conditions that make it possible for us to feel that we can cope with whatever comes up in performance and in our lives. We can trust that we shall be able to perform even if we have adrenaline in the system – we can let go of being frightened of being frightened.

How do you feel in your concerts?

It is good to see your emotional response to a concert situation as a habit, an automatic unchosen response, something that can be identified and worked on. The most important element of performance to understand and have in your control is *your emotional state*. It does not matter how much practice you have done, if your performance anxiety ruins your performance. If you have good teaching and practice well and have experience of playing with others you can develop an excellent instrumental and ensemble technique. It is easy enough to have a thorough knowledge of the repertoire but then find you lack mental clarity in the concert. You can easily find that your technique, reliable enough in the practice room, is not reliable in the concert hall. If you are anxious and tense you cannot draw on your reserves of developed skill!

How do you feel after your concerts?

Maybe, after the concert you feel you have underperformed; you *know* you could have played better. What should you do after such a concert?

The truth of the matter is you could not have played any better than you did in that concert. It is simply true that we always play as well as we can in concerts. You bring everything you have *at your disposal at that time* and play however you do. For it to be otherwise you would have had to be in a position to, and prepared to, do something different. It is certainly true to say that we can improve our chances next time, but the last time was as good as it could have been and the same will be the case after the next performance; you will have played as well as you could then as well. If you take this home truth on board you are releasing yourself from the imaginary vagaries of luck or fate deciding how you play in concerts and accepting you can make a difference to the performance as it happens.

- It is the quality of your overall state, your thinking, your emotional state, your internal/external awareness and in particular your freedom to react to whatever happens outside your control during the concert that makes the difference. You can have Conscious Control of yourself but not of someone dropping their programme, stuff happens!

A disappointing performance often generates a lot of intense practice, however it is not very important to practise instrumental technique or revise your knowledge of the repertoire, unless you really were underprepared (the disappointment would suggest you were prepared). You should prioritize how to transform your performance anxiety.

How is your Primary Control?

The Primary Control (Chapter 5) is always of critical importance when dealing with performance anxiety. To find out what is going on in the Primary Control you ask yourself suitable questions.

- Are you setting or fixing your head in a position?
- Are you pushing your head forward in space?
- Are you lifting your chin?
- Is your head moveable and rebalancing on the top of the spine?
- Are you pulling your head back and down or are you releasing your head forwards and up?
- Can you notice the tendency for the sternocleidomastoid muscles to give an effortless lightness to the front of the body, as the head tips forward?
- Are you directing your head forwards and up in such a way that the back is lengthening and widening?

Slow onset startle pattern

The startle pattern (see pp. 36–8) is an automatic response built into all of us; chemicals are released into the system to increase the blood pulse and when we start breathing again we breathe shallower and faster, this makes us more powerful and alert. This is all useful if we are going to have to escape from a burning building but not such a good state if we are going to play a concert. Performance anxiety excites the same reactions in us but the onset is slower. The extra power can reduce subtle control and the alertness tends to be overfocused on the danger, that is, the worry about the concert. In short we are overexcited. If, on the day of a concert, you notice the developing symptoms, you have a chance of cutting off the chain of events. Self-observation allows you to intervene in your responses consciously and starting with freeing your neck, you can break the chain of reactions, leaving yourself calm, confident and more in control of the situation.

Are you in balance?

When you are experiencing performance anxiety you will, almost certainly, have lost the freedom in your body's balancing reflexes (Chapter 15). Think of people who are frightened, they often look like 'a rabbit in the headlights'. If your instrumental technique includes skilful balance between you and the instrument when you are practising it is vital that you can take that free balancing into performance. If you are not rebalancing freely it will feel unfamiliar and that will increase performance anxiety. If you notice you are not free to rebalance, *that* is worth your attention; 'direct' your head and notice the weight on your feet; look for movement throughout your body. As you improve your sense of balance you will reduce your performance anxiety. Holding yourself in 'good posture' is not free rebalancing.

- If you are anxious, check that you are free to rebalance.
- If you are standing, after considering the Primary Control the next place to consider is your ankles.

- Remember (from Chapter 9: Body Mapping) that the ankle joint is where your leg articulates with the foot, not the back of your foot.
- If you are sitting, after considering the Primary Control the next places to consider are sitting bones and hip joints.

Are you breathing?

It is accurate to say that you cannot be nervous when you are breathing normally, in fact you will feel normal if you breathe normally! Unnecessary tension has the affect of shifting the breathing movement higher in the thorax so it becomes more frequent and shallower, typical nervous breathing! (See Chapter 10: Breathing.)

Ask the following constructive questions:

- Am I holding extra tension in the abdominal wall as air comes into my lungs?
- Are the ribs moving freely, moving like bucket handles articulating at the spine and the sternum?
- Are the back of my nose and throat open to allow free breathing?
- Am I holding tension in my throat?

How does your voice sound?

If you are anxious it will affect your voice. It is something you will notice in your friends if they are anxious. You can work on enjoying the full resonance of your voice when you are not anxious: that skill will be useful on the day of a concert. If you introduce pieces in your concerts, you have a perfect opportunity to enjoy the resonance of your voice, reducing performance anxiety as you talk. Think of speaking to people at the back and sides of the hall and notice how your voice bounces off the walls. Sense the way your whole body vibrates when you speak to a large audience, if you get the audience laughing you will almost certainly feel more at ease (see Chapter 11: Voice).

- If your voice is resonant you will feel more confident.
- If you are a singer, vocal resonance will be a great source of confidence.

Do you wear blinkers for concerts?

Another typical expression of anxiety is tightening the eyes. When you see a friend before a concert you know if they are nervous; their eyes might be overfocused or glazed over. If you realize that you have lost awareness of your environment through overfocus you can change the picture by directing your attention to your peripheral vision; this will help you to feel less anxious. See in depth and notice movement – check that you are blinking. It is possible to direct your visual system to improve your performance (see Chapter 12: Vision, for more detail).

- Get interested in your eyes being flexible, like the rest of the body, they are designed to move.

What about a lie down?

If you are experiencing performance anxiety and you are having trouble restoring a suitable equilibrium, it is often very helpful to use semi-supine (Chapter 13). It can be powerful practice, when lying in semi-supine, to imagine a place where you have been happy and easy with yourself. This might be in your garden, in the park, walking in the hills or on a beach. Notice how this helps your body to release and your breathing to be easy.

- Allow gravity to work gently on your muscles that are expressing anxiety.
- Thoughtfully scan your body for tension. When you have thought your way round the body you will probably be feeling more secure and confident.

- Stay lying down but visualize leaving semi-supine and warming up on your instrument and then walking on stage and starting to play. Appreciate the easy relationship between your head and spine as you play.
- Visualizing the upcoming performance while you are experiencing the freedom and confidence of your psychophysical state in semi-supine will make freedom and confidence more available in the actual performance: the more you practise it, the more it will permeate your performances.

Do you use your imagination?

The stories about Fritz Kreisler are inspirational. He was capable of making extraordinary use of imagination. My favourite Kreisler story is about a trip from London to Manchester on the train. He had not learnt the concerto he was going to play with the orchestra that day, so he studied the score on the journey. At the rehearsal, that afternoon, he played from memory!! He exuded confidence in performance – he was prepared for anything. We might not be able to match that feat of memory but we can make use of mental preparation to exude confidence.

- Imagine yourself in the room in which you are going to perform, playing beautifully and accurately with free balanced Use, enjoying yourself – you are reinforcing the likelihood of that happening.
- If you are imagining a negative scenario, you are reinforcing that likelihood.
- Bring all of your senses into play when you are using imagination.
- See the room around you with your colleagues, the instruments and the audience.
- Smell the polish on the floor of the stage.
- Hear the music and notice the acoustic (easier if you have played there before).

- Taste that little piece of chocolate you ate just before you came on stage.
- Feel the stage under your feet and the rest of your body rebalancing above your feet.
- Sense the freedom in your Primary Control.
- Sense the resistance of your instrument.
- Imagine dealing easily with the unpredictable nature of your colleagues' playing and any noises from the audience or outside the concert hall.
- See yourself in balance, calm and confident.
- In short, imagine an enjoyable performance.

How to let go of tension

When we are nervous we express it with tension, often in critical muscles where we need fine motor control. Trumpet players might create lip tension or wobble; violinists might lift the shoulders and tighten arm and hand muscles; organists might lose freedom in the hips. First, you need to be aware of your pattern. Ask yourself if there is unnecessary tension around, especially in areas you have found it in the past. Bring your attention to your symptoms of nervousness – accepting them starts to transform them. If you try to ignore them or just hope they will go away you are not taking control of the situation. If you ignore a problem it often festers away in the background and rears its ugly head at the wrong moment. Accept that the negative emotion is your habit but know that you can change it. When you recognize a negative pattern, create a positive Directional thought that counteracts it.

- Use Direction to contradict any negative pattern.
- We can express performance anxiety before or during a concert – it is appropriate to work on transforming this state in all circumstances.

Can you sense what you are doing to yourself?

At first, Alexander could not sense what he was doing to himself in performance that was causing his voice problems. That scenario is a normal human condition. Be interested to sense what you do to yourself when you express performance anxiety (or tension in your daily life). It took Alexander months, if not years to come to terms with this. With help, from an Alexander teacher, it is possible to make rapid progress. Ask yourself, what is going on, now? Keep your curiosity level high. If you sense what you are doing you have a chance of changing it. You are working on improving your relationship with your sensory feedback.

If your lips are wobbling

- Bring your attention your Primary Control and breathing first.
- Free your tongue when it is not involved in playing.
- Let gravity affect your jaw.
- Notice any other tension in your face – do you need that?
- Notice what you are doing in your throat – direct your throat to soften.
- Enjoy the sensation in your lips while playing.

If you are raising your shoulders unnecessarily

- Work on your Primary Control and breathing first.
- Allow your shoulders to widen away from each other.
- Allow the arms to be free at the sternoclavicular joints.
- Direct your elbows away from your shoulders to encourage your shoulders to release.

Are your arms and hands tense?

It is worth asking yourself, 'am I tensing my hands?' Some musicians walk around as if they are carrying something, arms flexed and hands closing on nothing. If you notice this happening before playing you will immediately improve the situation just by noticing it. If you are noticing your arms and hands not working in a coordinated way during the concert, it is tempting to try harder to play well – this will probably make the situation worse. It is better to think some key Directions: Primary Control, breathing, balance and let the hands lead the arms. This indirect approach addresses your anxiety, frees your arms and accesses the skill you have developed in practice.

When do you feel comfortable?

Many of us feel most comfortable and least nervous *when we are communicating well* so that should be our aim in a concert. Just imagine going to a party and finding you don't know anyone there; you feel uncomfortable. When do you start feeling comfortable? – Often when you start talking to someone and feel you are communicating! It is a good strategy to talk to your friends and colleagues, in fact anyone, before a concert, if the alternative is to focus on being nervous! Some people do feel better being quiet and on their own; make sure you know which camp you are in. If you allow yourself to be aware of your colleagues, in the concert, your interaction with them will make you, and them, more comfortable. The opposite would be desperately hanging on to playing your part as well as you can.

- When you include the audience in your consciousness, communication on a grand scale takes place.
- Your body language is communicating something from the moment you step into the audience's vision.
- Working on your Use works indirectly on your body language.

- Introduce the pieces verbally to the audience whenever possible; it can help relieve your performance anxiety.
- You may be able to sense the audience is listening to you, when you are playing, that is their part of the communication.

Are you present in your concerts?

If you are practising the concert repertoire just before you go on, you plant the idea that you are not ready for the concert and that will take you away from your confidence. The time to focus on the concert is during the concert, not before it. Being in the present is a part of being a good performer and part of the solution to performance anxiety. Thinking about how you played the next passage last time is not being present. If you are anticipating the 'difficult' section coming up soon, you are not in the present. We find a lot of students are reluctant to play to each other. Practise playing to your friends and relatives, just one person makes all the difference, you can practise being present while you play to them. If there are no friends or relatives available, a recording device can make a reasonable substitute.

- Talk to the audience, you will set up a rapport and feel their presence.
- Learn the pieces before the day of the concert.
- Don't anticipate problems – you have prepared.
- Commit to what you are doing now.
- See what's going on around you.
- Feel your relationship with gravity and your instrument.
- Perform to your friends and relatives.

Are you judgemental of other musicians?

It is easier to believe the audience is not there with the intention of judging you if you do not go to other musicians' concerts in that frame of mind yourself. When you are listening to concerts, take part actively just as you would wish from your audiences; be interested in the communication. Remember that you do not have to be the world's best player nor even the best player of your instrument in the room, to be worth being heard. It is not a competition when you play a concert. Remember that your best experiences in other musicians' concerts are when the performers communicate the composer's and their own musical intentions to you.

- Don't be judgemental in other musicians' concerts.
- Don't turn a concert into a competition, whether you are playing or listening.
- Music is a game for playing not for winning.

What performance are you preparing for?

When you are preparing for a performance you are preparing for any eventuality. If you have prepared the 'perfect performance' you will almost certainly be put off your stroke by something external or internal. You need a great deal of flexibility in a performance – performance anxiety eats away at your flexibility. You limit yourself if you prepare an ideal rendition. When you find the performance moving away from your ideal you can suffer anxiety. The trouble seems to be that you are actually trying to live in the past, to play the way you did in rehearsal or practice. That way might have been ideal then but this is now. Interactivity and communication are what are required now; remove the straightjacket of a preplanned performance and create a unique performance now in the present. You will be reducing performance anxiety the more you are prepared to be flexible. If you play competitive sports or games you will probably understand the need for the ability to deal with whatever is thrown at you. Fortunately, in a concert, your colleagues are not trying to make things difficult for you but for whatever reason, they will occasionally bowl you a googly, to use a cricketing metaphor (a curve ball if you prefer baseball). You will be doing the same to them and the way to avoid increased anxiety when it happens to be balanced and poised in such a way that you can move musically and psychophysically in any Direction at any time.

- Don't prepare the perfect performance.
- Prepare to be flexible musically and psychophysically.
- Anything might or might not happen.

Summary

- What are you afraid of?
- You always play your best!
- If you breathe normally you feel normal.
- Release your abdominal muscles.
- Use semi-supine before the concert.
- Listen to the quality of your voice.
- Primary Control is, as usual, of prime importance.
- Where is your tension?
- See the room around you.
- Use all your senses.
- Use your imagination.
- Address your particular fears with the Means-whereby.
- Communicate with your colleagues and the audience.
- Learn the pieces before the day of the concert!
- Be happy to be present.
- Don't be judgemental.
- Be interested in free balance.
- Anything might or might not happen.

Student quotes

At the start of my Final Recital, I was aware that I was falling into my usual habits so before playing, I took a moment's pause to stop, breathe and choose consciously how to respond to the stimulus of being nervous on stage. I directed my head forwards and up allowing my spine to fall away from my primary control so that my back could lengthen and widen. Choosing how to react to the nervous situation allowed me to feel present within my body and gave me a sense of ownership on stage.

Felicity Matthews, viola player

I really enjoyed the tips we learned about the importance of thinking about breathing normally in remaining calm on stage. The idea that you have always done as much as you can to prepare for a performance given the other choices you made (e.g. having to see friends, go shopping etc.) really struck a chord with me as I sometimes feel as if we are expected to do nothing with our lives but what our degree demands.

Georgia Scott, composer

CHAPTER TWENTY-THREE

Preparing for powerful performance

Preparing for powerful performance

Because the principle is general in its application, a musician is learning something he can use to advantage in whatever he is doing. And conversely, his improved Use of himself in everyday life will be reflected in his music.[1]

Learn the pieces

It is a good idea to learn the pieces before the concert. This might sound obvious but if your habit is to learn the pieces thoroughly – let yourself accept that you have, it will improve your performance. If your habit is to think that you have underprepared, however much you have done (this seems to be a very common habit), it will undermine your performance. Some students tend to practise the parts of a piece they find easy rather than those they find problematic, this is obviously a negative habit as far as preparing for performance.

Should you practice more?

Your life is full of choices. You cannot spend all your time practising; in fact, that would be poor preparation for playing concerts because your playing would lack essential life experience that will inform your performances. We have to see clearly that we are continuously making choices: if we make choices that prepare us for our concerts, we will be ready. If you want to spend more time preparing for concerts you might choose to spend travelling time with the scores, or record your practice and listen to it when you are travelling.

At the RCM we have a room set up as a 'Virtual Concert Hall'. There is a Green Room where you can hear the virtual audience (a filmic projection) waiting for you to enter; you walk into the performing space to their applause and they react to your performance in every way that a real audience might. This is a great asset for practising performing for our students. If you develop the skill of imagining the experience of playing the upcoming

[1]Jones, *Awareness, Freedom and Muscular Control.*

concert that you are preparing for, you can have a similar 'virtual reality' experience. It helps if you include as much sensory detail as possible. You can set up the feeling you are playing the concert for the second time when your real concert happens. When you are playing the virtual reality concerts include free Primary Control, balance, flexible breathing and seeing in depth; you will be practising putting those qualities in place for the actual concert. These virtual reality concerts will let you know where you are underprepared; that is useful for when you have your next playing practice time.

Practising in the clothes (including shoes) you will wear in concerts is sensible. First you find out if you can move freely in them and second you can more easily imagine playing the concert, in 'concert dress'.

Run up and down stairs

A friend of ours who had a very high profile concert in the offing, told us of an interesting strategy. She is a flute player and knew that she would have more rapid breathing and pulse when the big obligato arrived. She practised for it by running up and down stairs until she was out of breath, and then played through the movement. This was very good preparation because when she found she could cope even when her breathing and heartbeat were challenged, she became more confident that all would be okay on the day. Doubtless that confidence meant that she was less put out of kilter when the time came. We heard the concert and it was confident, beautiful and in total control. In this way, to a significant extent, you can practise being nervous!

Be there – at the rehearsals

It is obvious that some musicians are physically present at the rehearsal but their attention is somewhere else. You can bring yourself into the present in rehearsal by noticing your Primary Control, breathing and vision as well as how you are playing.

Being 'present' implies full interactivity with the other players. You can practise being present at any time in your daily life, which is good practice for performance.

Problem corners

It may seem an obvious thing to say but, if you are not clear about a corner of the piece during the rehearsal it could be an anxious moment for you in the concert; is it your habit to clarify the situation or not? We find some students would rather keep their head down in a rehearsal than mention that they are finding a corner unclear. If you get to the concert with an unavoidable lack of clarity remaining, aim to have a free neck, keep breathing and keep seeing panoramically when those corners arrive; if you make that plan in advance it is more likely to be possible when the time comes.

Be genuine

We would all like to be thought of as 'good performers'. A good performer is someone who communicates well with the other performers and the audience. There is no contrivance or pretence involved in good performance, rather a revealing of your relationship with the music. Your interpretation does not have to be the 'best version of the piece ever' to be worth hearing. If you are totally genuine the audience will respond. We find there is a performer inside all musicians – it is good to acknowledge that part of you that wants to perform – we all need to find our 'Diva'! You can ask yourself the question 'am I doing anything that is getting in the way of revealing what I feel and think about this music?'

Power through flexibility

A musician becomes a powerful performer when they find flexibility. Their power does not come from building up tension and there is very little need for absolute strength.

Staying psychophysically aware helps avoid anxiety creeping in unnoticed; this helps us to maintain our flexibility, confidence and coordination. We are undoing any 'startle pattern' that might be a reaction to the performance.

Be aware that the performance has started when the audience first sees you; do you hide behind the formality of bowing (that lacks flexibility) or do you connect with the audience? Before you walk on stage and as you walk on, you can find panoramic vision, free breathing and balance to help you connect with the audience before you start playing, as well as during the performance.

Your daily life style

You have a better chance of performing well if you have enough sleep and eat healthy food. It is worth seeing that your choices of food and drinks become habitual over time. If your habits are healthy you have made good choices that will help you prepare for performance. RCM research in the Centre for Performing Science shows that a certain level of physical fitness reduces performance anxiety and improves stamina for playing concerts.

Warm-up

Some musicians find semi-supine a good way to compose themselves for performance, although most musicians benefit from being upright and engaged, for a few minutes, before the performance starts.

- If you are tired – lying in semi-supine for 10 minutes can re-energize you if you are not too exhausted.

Other musicians find a series of gentle movements away from their instrument an ideal warm-up for concerts. Tai Chi or Chi Kung can be used in just this way. It is the quality of the movements that make them valuable.

Ask yourself, 'What do you want from your warm-up?' Tailor it to suit.

Just before the concert

We all need to find our best way of preparing just before a concert but it is worth bearing a few ideas in mind.

- It helps to be interactive in the concert. Ask yourself, 'Does it help you to be interactive before the concert?'

- Be present rather than involved in detailed analysis or mental chatter.
- Less judgement more awareness.
- Are you balanced, are you breathing, are you seeing the room around you?
- Freshen up your reflex-facilitated approach to playing in your warm-up.
- Use Direction.
- Beware of contracting your body – let go and be expansive!
- A series of gentle movements can be a good warm-up.
- Some people find it best to be quiet before the performance.
- If you find yourself chatting and maybe even sharing a joke with a friend before you go on you are preparing for a confident communicative performance.

Student quotes

One of the things I am learning about acting in opera is that it is more powerful to let myself be a character than to try to be a character. I am learning that in order to do this, a great starting point is finding as neutral a state as possible, where my physical and emotional bodies are as quiet and effort-free as I dare let them be. Working with AT helps me notice finer physical, emotional and mental tension or gripping that I can begin to let go of.

Chris Ainslie, singer

(Poppy writing about a series of movements that she uses as a preparation for performances)

To do these movements well, it is necessary to really think clearly, with Direction, and not to 'zone out' visually or be caught up in our associative thoughts. I find that whilst I perform these movements I am brought more into the present moment. If I am nervous about that particular concert situation, for example a live radio broadcast, then this presence helps me interrupt that stage fright – the startle pattern. After these preparations, I feel that I walk on stage already open, well-coordinated, and with an expanded field of attention so necessary for orchestral playing. My arms are 'light', activated and sensitive: ready to be a channel to the instrument. I'm more available to respond, take risks, and be vivid musically.

Poppy Walshaw, cellist and Alexander teacher

CHAPTER TWENTY-FOUR

Enhanced ensemble skills

What distinguishes the Alexander Technique from all other methods of self improvement that I know anything about is the character of the thinking involved. To me it is an expansion of the field of attention in space and in time so that you are taking in both yourself and your environment, both the present moment and the next. It is a unified field organized around the self as a centre.[1]

The Schubert Ensemble at King's Place London

[1]Jones, *Learning How to Learn.*

Ensemble playing includes many varied challenges. Alexander work develops a broad range of awareness that will improve a musician's ensemble skills.

Internal awareness

We develop awareness of our internal freedom or lack of it. Our Primary Control, balance on the chair, the connection and balance with our instrument benefit from our awareness of them. The sensory feedback through the nervous system keeps us in touch with how we are controlling the instrument; we are sensing how we are playing. We can also be aware of our emotional responses and how they might be affecting our playing.

External awareness

It is obviously necessary to have awareness of the other musicians that we are playing with, so it is clear that a combined internal and external awareness is called for in ensemble playing. We understand very easily that it is possible to focus our attention on a detail; it is what we do in practice and in ensemble rehearsal if someone is making a point about a specific issue. It is common to focus by narrowing our attention and reducing awareness of everything else, leaving the spotlight bright on the object in mind. When playing through or performing in an ensemble we need quite a different state of mind and body; we need to broaden our attention to include more. The broadening usually expands our external awareness.

Expanded field of attention

We are not looking for a divided field of attention, internal and external. We are capable of choosing what we attend to by broadening our awareness into a more comprehensive state, some internal and some external. If we then decide to select one, two or three areas of special interest and give each about 10 per cent of our attention, we still have at least 70 per cent of our available awareness for the big picture and anything particularly interesting that might develop into a new priority. Overfocus on playing our instrument is a problem as it takes us out of the group that we are playing in. If we think of instrumental technique to the exclusion of the ensemble, we cannot expect to play well with the others. Instrumental technique is something that can be included in our overall awareness but it is not due for focus at this time.

There is not a physical or mental boundary between the internal and the external; it is only a self-imposed restriction if we decide there is. The way to improve the expanded field of attention is to practise it.

As you read this book practise combining internal and external awareness. Sense your feet on the ground; notice the room around you while you notice what you are reading.

> Information about the state of the body and the state of the environment is being recorded in the brain at one and the same time.[2]

Some practical applications

Starting together

---

[2]Jones, *Organisation of Awareness*, p. 7.

Starting together

When two or more chamber musicians need to start together, an Alexander approach can help. We are not trying hard to play together. We are allowing ourselves to be present with our Primary Control, balance and breathing, our vision, our sense of how to play our instrument in the style required, our memory of the tempo we have agreed on in rehearsal and a corporate sense of movement. That sentence took a long time to read but this awareness can all happen in a moment. We feel physical contact with our instrument and the preparing of conditions in mind and body for playing the opening passage. We observe the movement of the other members of the group, especially the person 'leading' and we join in the movement that we are all making together to start playing at the agreed tempo that the leader has reconfirmed in their initial gesture.

It is not easy to move precisely after being static, starting playing from static leads to less reliable ensemble. For this reason all members of the group move together before making a sound to facilitate ensemble. Every member of the group then feels they are part of the starting gesture and so part of the leading movement, whether they are the designated 'leader' or not. Ideally, every player is in panoramic vision taking in the corporate sense of movement.

- What we are not looking for is everyone except the leader, sitting rigid with tension, not breathing, with eyes boring into the leader, seeing when the leader starts and trying as hard as possible to play at the same time.
- All human gestures start with a tensional shift in the relationship between the head and the spine, the Primary Control; if all players have reflex-facilitated balance, free breathing and flexible Primary Control, it will be easy to communicate and start together.

Exceptional timing

There is a quality that is recognized in many different fields. It is a quality of poise, gracefulness and coordination in activity.

Thinking of cricketers the first example that springs to mind is the batting of David Gower. Commentators often said, 'he seems to have more time to play his shots than other batsmen.' Whether Gower was aware of his Primary Control or not, he demonstrated superbly coordinated Primary Control; that helped him to size up the situation that was developing as the cricket ball came towards him, sometimes at more than 90 miles an hour and with a languid gesture would stroke the ball away to the boundary with perfect timing and the minimum of effort. The same is true of great musicians on all instruments, they are unhurried but can play very quickly or slowly, with the minimum of effort; they meet the next musical gesture with perfect timing and seem in total control of the situation. How many times have you heard the audience leaving a virtuoso performance saying, 'and she made it look so easy!'? It is visually obvious even to the untrained eye when the Primary Control and the overall balance in a musician are working well; it looks skilful and easy. It is very easy to play with a musician who has 'David Gower' timing and balance, as the visual cues are crystal clear.

The three questions

Are we compromising our ensemble skills? At any time you can think in activity to refresh your awareness.

The three questions are useful for all activities – ensemble playing is no exception.

1. Am I balancing?
2. Am I breathing?
3. Am I seeing the room around me?

How to use your hearing

Hearing is not useful for starting together but it is very useful for assessing the tempo, dynamic, tonal quality and style that are on-going in the performance. It will also tell you, retrospectively, if you started together but, of course you are too late to change that. When you are playing you can make many assessments by listening but it is good to sense your instrument, its vibrations and your movements because they can help you play differently in the present.

When you are considering instrumental balance it is easy to think that your hearing will be the resource to draw on but only someone separate from their instrument can really hear the balance. A player in the group who is not playing has a better idea but someone in the auditorium will find it easy – you can rely on their hearing of the group as a whole. If someone you trust goes to the auditorium during your rehearsal and suggests any adjustments to balance that are necessary, you will then be in a position to judge how to play by using your sense of the vibrations from your instrument within the ensemble's resonance. That proprioceptive feedback is most reliable for adjusting the balance from then on. 'Perception' is to do with the environment – 'proprioception', the body. Your proprioception is very useful for intonation in much the same way. In some passages, on some instruments, it is not possible to hear yourself play; you can always feel what is going on and that can become very reliable, but only if you spend time developing the skill.

- Your proprioception is vital in ensemble playing.

Interactivity

Accept anything that happens or does not happen. Even if we are playing our part 'perfectly', there may well be problems to deal with. Playing in an ensemble is interactive and if we have an idea of playing our part perfectly that is not related to the rest of the group's playing we are not acknowledging that basic truth. If you are playing in the 'right place' and everyone else is playing in a different place, it is questionable if you really are in the right place. The same can, of course, be said about volume, style, attack, intonation, and so on. In fact, we are barking up the wrong tree, if we think we might play perfectly. It is putting us into a straightjacket and that will always be uncomfortable. So whatever happens, accept it and respond using all of your available potential. To increase your potential, free your neck, allow continuous rebalancing, be curious about your awareness and enjoy being interactive with your colleagues and the environment.

Student quotes

I realized I could actually tell how my chamber music partners were feeling in the way they were holding their bodies. I was surprised I had never noticed these things before. After studying the Alexander Technique, I feel much more 'in control of the situation' when I am playing. I am able to be spontaneous in phrasing, character and timing in a performance now and feel less scared of hard passages. I am also more prepared to receive criticism and use it constructively.

Miranda Barritt, cellist

Another habit of mine, that I have noticed, is that I tend to frown or look concerned when I play. This not only creates tension in my face and therefore in my body overall but it must also give signals to other people that I am worried and anxious about playing as well as signalling to myself that I am anxious and uncomfortable with the situation.

Hannah Masson-Smyth, cellist

Conclusion

We have written this book because we have seen how useful Alexander's ideas can be for a musician's self-development. It is obvious to us that the Technique is a catalyst in the learning process; in fact it could be described as a way of 'learning how to learn'. To a certain extent we have to do what Alexander did. We strip away layers of negative habit of mind, body and emotional attitude to reveal an in-built reliable coordination. We can then bring our newly reliable coordination to everything we do.

Understanding the relationship between skill and habit helps us to constantly refine our skills both technical and musical. Understanding the central nature of habit in our lives helps us to accept who we are and choose how to handle change. We become more present and consciously aware of what it is to play our instrument and play music with other people. We develop a toolkit of ideas for dealing with all our musical challenges that enhances our ability to practise and perform. We find more possibility of being creative, genuine and spontaneous in performance.

This practical philosophy can help us to be wide awake and in a state of open curiosity that makes it a greater pleasure to be involved in the wonderful human activity of playing music.

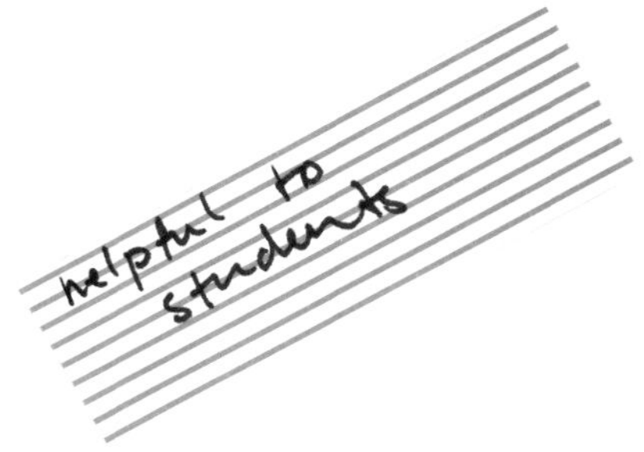

BIOGRAPHIES OF F. M. ALEXANDER, F. P. JONES AND DR W. BARLOW

F. M. Alexander 1869–1955

Frederick Matthias Alexander was an actor, born in Tasmania. The ideas that he developed, 'Alexander Principles', evolved from his practical experience and difficulties as a performer. All his life he had a great love of the theatre and in particular of Shakespeare. He studied in Melbourne with eminent teachers of the day and immersed himself in the theatre and cultural life.

By the age of 22 he was performing but suffering from hoarseness and loss of voice. His friends told him, they could hear him gasping for air during his solo Shakespearean recitations. The doctor's advice to rest only gave him temporary relief, so in search of a solution to the problem with his voice he began to observe and analyse how he was reciting.

After self-observation he managed to solve his vocal problems and in the process developed his principles that can be applied to all human activities. His reputation as a performer rose, as did his reputation as a teacher who could help other performers with various problems. He directed and took part in performances of plays, including Hamlet and Merchant of Venice, with many of his pupils as the cast.

He moved with his immediate family in 1904 to London, taking his teaching discoveries to a wider public. This was a very positive move; London was a supportive environment for people with new ideas. He became well known in London society with his clientele coming from all walks of life such as performers, writers, politicians, scientists and doctors; Sir Henry Irvine, Sir Adrian

Boult, George Bernard Shaw, Aldous Huxley, Sir Stafford Cripps and Dr Wilfred Barlow, to name a few.

With the outbreak of the First World War, he found he had fewer pupils and decided to move to New York – he felt it was very important to continue to teach and develop his ideas. His practice was soon flourishing in this new environment and over the next ten years he lived about eight months of the year in New York and returned for the summers in London, where his brother AR was keeping the teaching practice going while he was abroad. One of his new pupils, John Dewey, an educational philosopher and prime mover in the American education system, saw the Alexander Technique as a great contribution to the field of Education. He wrote, 'The Alexander Technique bears the same relationship to education that education bears to all human activities.'

In 1924, a school for 3–8-year-old children was opened at Alexander's studios in Victoria, London. In 1934, the 'Little School' moved to Penhill in Kent, Alexander's country house. Irene Tasker ran the school using the conventional curriculum but based the teaching on Alexander's principles. The Second World War saw the school move to the United States for the safety of the children. The school was not re-established in the United Kingdom although Alexander's ideas have been incorporated into the life of some schools, for example currently, Educare in Kingston Upon Thames, Surrey, UK.

Alexander wrote four books setting out his ideas and how he saw the state of the human race. The first was published in 1910, the last in 1941. There are now a great many books written about the Technique, as exponents set out 'the principles' in contemporary style, looking at making connections with their particular area of interest (this being an example). There are also biographies of Alexander's long and fascinating life.

He had trained his brother Albert Redden and his sister Amy to teach his Technique.

Many of Alexander's students expressed an interest in training to teach the Technique. He started training the first group in 1930. The training of new teachers to continue his work and expand its reach was seen, especially by the trainees, as essential to his legacy. Many of his acolytes went on to open their own training courses.

Alexander had a stroke in his late seventies but made a full recovery by applying his principles throughout his convalescence.

The strength of his teaching was increased by the absolute necessity for his Direction to be the source of his strength as his physical body was in a weakened state. People who had lessons between that time and his death in 1955 said his teaching was at its highest level during these last years.

Alexander's legacy includes the many Alexander teachers and teacher training schools all over the World. His Technique is now taught in the music colleges in Britain and many conservatories in Europe, America, Japan and Australia, also in specialist music schools for younger students as well as university departments. There are many books looking at the Technique in relation to music. Many eminent musicians swear by the work, saying it has helped them in many significant ways.

He was said to have been a loveable rogue, not an entirely angelic man; we rather like that about him. Alexander was described as a charismatic man; he inspired many great men and women to adopt a new approach to living their lives. Many of them wrote about the ideas and devoted their energy to supporting his work. He always loved horses and betting on horse races. He was known to enjoy a glass of wine or two, which endears him to many a professional musician.

F. M. Alexander was an extraordinary visionary man and educator; many of us see him as one of the geniuses of the twentieth century. He looked at the human condition and did not accept it as immutable. He passed on his insight and thanks to him and those he taught, thousands of lives are being improved by the use of his Principles. Alexander's Technique is a profound contribution to the understanding of human potential, movement, education, health and, our special interest, the performing arts.

Frank Pierce Jones 1905–75

Ted Dimon (Alexander teacher, writer and publisher of the collected writings of Frank Pierce Jones) describes FPJ as 'a true renaissance man, inventive with an enquiring spirit and high standards of excellence.' We have been inspired to include Jones's biography and quote from his articles and book because of his beautiful writing on the Alexander Technique in relation to musicians and music making, which has influenced our thinking and teaching.

F. P. Jones was born in Appleton, Wisconsin. As a child he suffered with asthma and allergies and in his twenties with TB. He studied classics and went on to become a professor of Psychology at Tufts University. Having read about Alexander's work in Aldous Huxley's *Ends and Means* he took a course of lessons with A. R. Alexander (FM's brother). In 1937, he went on to have a series of lessons with FM. As his health improved so much he was inspired to train to be an Alexander teacher, his wife also trained.

He describes a little of his first lesson:

> the act of rising out of a chair, which I had always performed so laboriously before, was being done for me by a set of reflex machinery whose operation I knew nothing about, everything I did became easier.

His appreciation of the experience he received in Alexander lessons shows him to be an open minded 'academic'. He became particularly interested in Alexander's Principle of Psychophysical Unity and its influence on attention and awareness.

He began to see that Alexander's work had real scientific merit and hoped like FM it would become universally accepted and therefore widely available to those who needed it. In 1949 he embarked on his quest to demonstrate the scientific validity, through research and writing, of FM's discovery in a clear and comprehensible way. During his time as professor of Psychology at Tufts University, he worked with many musicians. He wrote a book, *Freedom to Change* (The Development and Science of the Alexander Technique) and various short pamphlets on the Technique. His writing for musicians focuses on freewill (or spontaneity) and making the connection between conscious awareness and attention in performance.

Dr Wilfred Barlow 1915–91

Born in the north of England and bought up in North Wales, Barlow was a considerable athlete, playing tennis at county level and representing Oxford University.

After a skiing injury he had lessons with FM and went on to train to be an Alexander teacher. He married FM's niece Marjory, also an Alexander teacher. He did a huge amount to promote the Alexander Technique in the medical world and undertook ground breaking research at the Central School of Speech (now, the Central School of Speech and Drama) and the RCM. He wrote two books *The Alexander Principle* (1973) and *More Talk of Alexander* (1978). His books show his interest in a broad spectrum of areas including the medical, in which the Technique is very effective and he was particularly interested in the influence of the emotional state on a person's Use.

He championed FM's work all his life and set up the Alexander Institute, becoming its medical advisor.

We have included him and his work because of his research and great contribution to the understanding of the Technique, his strong connection with the RCM and through that link to the music world at large.

THE DEVELOPMENT OF THE ALEXANDER TECHNIQUE AT THE ROYAL COLLEGE OF MUSIC

In our opinion, this approach is the best means we have yet encountered for solving the artist's problem of communication and should form the basis of his training.[1]

RCM Vocal Profs

The authors outside the Royal College of Music – London

[1]Wilfred Barlow, *More Talk of Alexander*, Gollancz, London, 1978, p. 192.

The story starts in the early 1950s. Dr Wilfred Barlow and his wife Marjory (two Alexander teachers) were invited to run an experiment in the singing department at London's Royal College of Music. They gave a course of about 37 Alexander lessons to 50 students over a period of 3 months.The results were very impressive and a scientific comparison was made with a control group from the Central School of Speech.[2] The RCM singing professors produced written conclusions as follows.

> *In each case there has been a marked physical improvement, which was usually reflected vocally and dramatically. It was a revelation to discover that tricks of behaviour could be eliminated in a comparatively short space of time once the student learned to control his tensional balance from the head-neck region.*
>
> *In all cases students, since re-education, are easier to teach and can take and carry out stage Directions with greater ease. The students seem to become aware of themselves in a new way. Each student reacted in a different characteristic way. For example, those who had been over-anxious to please authority discovered that they could be themselves with impunity, ceasing to be such model students, but becoming better performers. One student, a girl hampered by angular stereotyped movements, and a curiously 'spinsterish' quality of personality, has acquired considerable warmth and gracefulness. Another, with originally a very mediocre 'drawing-room' voice, is now considered by her original teachers and critics to have developed the qualities of voice and personality that go to make a really great singer.*
>
> *The time it takes to get result varies greatly between one student and another. The utilization of the approach depends largely on the student himself.*
>
> *Eight of the fifty re-educated students entered last year for a singing prize which is competed for by women singers every four years. It is open to all amateur and professional singers under thirty years of age in the British Isles, and is considered the highest achievement possible for students. The total entry was over one hundred. Of the eight students who entered six*

---

[2]The comparative data is published in Barlow, *More Talk of Alexander*, pp. 98–9.

reached the semi-final, in which there were fifteen competitors. This is quite out of proportion to what one might expect.

In our opinion, this approach is the best means we have yet encountered for solving the artist's problem of communication and should form the basis of his training.

That inspirational final conclusion was followed up with the introduction of Alexander teaching at the RCM, not as 'the basis' of the education but at least it was made available to music students at a major international conservatory. The teachers giving these trail-blazing lessons were Joyce Wodeman, Joan Warrack and Adam Nott. The lessons were given as an extracurricula activity for students 'who were considered to need them'.

The Alexander teaching was still running on the same basis when we began teaching at the RCM in 1989. We started a campaign to have Alexander lessons introduced to the core curriculum and found most of the professors were strong advocates of the Technique. We ran our own experiment that discovered a great enthusiasm for Alexander lessons among students who *weren't* 'considered to need them'. Approval for a mandatory introductory course for all first-year students (now known as level 4) was given and that course has now been part of the curriculum for over 20 years.

The present courses

There are now courses at levels 4, 5 and 6 within the BMus undergraduate degree. These are all funded from within the core degree budget. Levels 5 and 6 are available to years 3 and 4 undergraduate students. Postgraduates can choose to take the level 6 course and they have level 7 courses, only available to them. We have continuously developed the courses over the years, responding to feedback from the students.

The Alexander Technique being embedded in the BMus course, means the degree is aimed at more than achieving good musical results – with the inclusion of Alexander lessons, the degree course expands its relevance to the whole 'self' of the musician. This means the RCM has a degree where you can not only learn how to play music at an extremely high level but also learn to look after yourself and develop an understanding of psychophysical health that improves your ability to perform consistently at your highest level.

The classes

Alexander classes are taken in groups of five or six students. This allows for 'hands-on work', and group discussion of the principles and the philosophy of the work. The students include self-reflection and come to understand that the way to achieve their full potential and find their unique place in the music world is to use their mind and body without negative patterns getting in the way.

All of the courses have a self-observational diary or report. It soon became clear to us that writing a diary makes it more likely that the students' Alexander thinking develops and their enthusiasm for the work grows.

Level 4

The first-year course is a ten-week introduction that covers the basics of the technique. The classes usually have five students and last 30 minutes. It is a broad-spectrum course that is intended to give students an impression of the potential of studying the Technique and so empowers them to elect the more advanced courses, when the time comes, with a clear idea of what they are choosing.

Level 5

Third and fourth year students can choose this course. The maximum class size is 6 students. The lessons are 75 minutes a week over the academic year (22 weeks). The content focuses on the students' application of the Alexander Principles to playing their instrument in all situations. They observe each other playing and discuss practice and performance strategies. They write a practice diary, an introduction to the Technique and an extended essay.

Level 6

Fourth-year students who have completed level 5 can take level 6. Postgraduate students with suitable previous experience of the Technique can elect to take this course. The groups are a maximum of 6 students. The lessons are 75 minutes a week over the academic year (22 weeks). The focus of the course is communication in performance with particular reference to developing stage presence and connection with colleagues and the audience. The written work is a collaborative research project, looking at a particular aspect of being a musician and a self-reflexive statement at the end of the course. Three video recordings are made during the course, one being a mock audition.

Level 7

Postgraduate students can choose this short course. It is either five 60-minute classes or ten 30-minute classes. This is a broad-spectrum intensive course. The students are expected to read around the subject between the classes to make the course work well. The students write a diary and an Alexander book review.

A new course

We have a new postgraduate course under construction. The course objective is for students to study the main treatises written about their instrument, search out the psychophysical advice and compare that with the Alexander principles, looking for congruence and contradictions. They will write a dissertation making observations from the treatises and write their own treatise on how to play their instrument from an Alexander perspective. These new treatises will be collected over the years and become a body of work available to RCM students in subsequent years.

Non-academic Alexander lessons at the RCM

The non-academic lessons continue the valuable practice set up after Dr Barlow's experiment in the 1950s. Students are interested in having lessons for all sorts of reasons. Many students with particular physical or musical challenges have managed to transform their approach to their studies through these lessons. Some students elect to take these lessons throughout their years at the RCM because they realize the technique has a great deal to offer musicians when it comes to finding extra refinement in their playing. They are either one-to-one or one-to-two lesson in 30-minute slots on a weekly basis. Alongside us giving these lessons is our highly gifted and experienced colleague Bethan Pugh.

We have had students going on from the RCM to train as Alexander teachers in the past 20 years. They will have a second career path developing that will continuously inform their career in music. RCM Alexander students are using their experience of the Technique to enhance their successful performing careers in countries all over the world.

Many of the current RCM staff have experience of the Technique and are great supporters of the work. Here are a couple of their backstories:

> *One of the first things my new Singing teacher at the RCM said to me was that he wanted to me to start Alexander Technique lessons as soon as possible and that he had already arranged things! At that time, I knew almost nothing about AT, but the little snippets I had gleaned inferred that it was a 'kind of therapy' and, like most of my peer group, I was less than happy with the implication that 'there was something wrong with me' and, thus, viewed the prospect of AT lessons with some resistance, suspicion and scepticism. All that changed, however, at my first session with Joyce Wodeman. What an inspiring lady; she possessed a wealth of experience of the theatre and singing worlds and I was fascinated by her explanation of the background to the Technique, Alexander's own experiences and how she had trained with him in Albert Court Mansions.*

From day one, I was 'hooked'. The early-morning sessions each Friday became the highlight of the week, not least because of the incredible feeling of well-being which they engendered. As I absorbed the ideas and began to be able to put them into practice, I noticed, too, the effect upon my vocal performance and stage skills. Magic!

If you haven't experienced AT, do so as soon as possible. I'm sure you won't regret it.

David Harpham, singer – Registry Officer,
Royal College of Music, London

I remain deeply indebted to my teacher Nona Liddell, who refused to take me on as a violin student unless I simultaneously started Alexander Technique lessons. She referred me to Wilfred Barlow and there my journey of being turned inside out began. The first shock was the discovery that violin playing had made one side of my rib cage higher than the other. The second was realising that there were skills available that could help me deal with what I felt was an irretrievable mind-body split. My regular Alexander teacher for many years, Cheryl Gardiner, warned me that lessons with her would change all aspects of my life. She was right. The clearest memory I have of working with her is of my body unravelling like spaghetti so that I could hardly sign the cheque at the end of the session. In violin terms this meant a new space for resonance opening up inside me, which was frightening as well as liberating. Both Cheryl and Nona insisted upon the importance of waiting physically upon a musical impulse, so that I was only allowed to pick up the violin or put bow to string when I was 'ready'. I am not sure I have always been able to live up to that musical revolution violinistically, but it has continued to affect my whole view of musical expression.

Professor Amanda Glauert, violinist – Director of
Programmes and Research, Royal College of Music, London

BIOGRAPHIES OF THE AUTHORS

Judith Kleinman

Judith trained as a musician at the Guildhall School of Music and Drama. As a professional double bass player Judith's posts have included working with Roger Norrington's London Classical Players, English National Opera, London Jupiter Orchestra and the City of London Sinfonia. Judith's freelance work includes having played with the London Symphony Orchestra and the Orchestra of the Age of Enlightenment. Her interest in being freer and more comfortable when playing and more at ease in performance led her to the worlds of Alexander and movement.

The work has also been key in recovering from accident injuries. Judith started by having lessons in movement and awareness with Jean Gibson and then had her first Alexander lessons with Elisabeth Waterhouse at the Guildhall. She went on to train to be an Alexander teacher with Mr Macdonald, Shoshanna Kaminitz and Walter Vaughn Jones in London. Judith has taken postgraduate studies with many Alexander teachers including Walter Carrington, Marjory Barstow, Meredith Page and Barbara Conable. She continues to learn from all her colleagues, friends and students in the Alexander community.

Judith Kleinman is now one of the Alexander teachers at the RCM, collaborating with Peter Buckoke on working with the music students there. She also teaches and runs the Alexander teaching at the Junior Royal Academy of Music. Judith is Assistant Head of Training at the London Centre for Alexander Teacher Training and teaches at Westminster Alexander Training Course. Judith teaches

'Alexander for Singers' at Dartington Summer School and has taught on many courses including National Youth Orchestra, LSSO youth scheme and the music scholars at Oxford University. She has co-written a book, 'Edukindness', about teaching the Alexander Technique to young people with Sue Merry, and has collaborated often with Sue, giving lectures and workshops on working with children and teenagers. She has collaborated with Penny O'Conner at her Alexander workshops on Alonissos in Greece.

Judith is interested in continuing to explore poise and movement and how they can enhance the lives and performance of musicians. She is also a teacher of Tai Chi, having trained with Michael Spink in London. Judith is married to Peter Buckoke and they have two sons.

Peter Buckoke

Peter runs the Alexander department at the RCM, London. He joined the RCM in 1989 when he was invited to become a professor of the Double Bass. He joined the Alexander teaching staff in 1990 and gradually took on the running of the department. He trained as an Alexander teacher with Eleanor and Peter Ribeaux in the 1980s. He teaches at the Alexander teacher training courses run by Refia Sacks and John Hunter in London.

Peter studied the double bass in London and Rome. He played as sub-principal in the orchestra of Teatro La Fenice in Venice and then English National Opera, London, in the 1970s. Since 1980 he has freelanced in London mostly playing chamber music and with Period Instrument groups. Peter is a founder member of the Schubert Ensemble of London, a piano and strings group – winners of the Royal Philharmonic Society's coveted award for Best Chamber Group. Peter is the man in the cabaret duo, *A Man a Woman and a Double Bass* with Lowri Blake, who sings and plays the cello.

Peter looks after several colonies of bees, sited in London, Oxfordshire and Wales.

Judith and Peter are married. They live in North London with their two sons, Harry and Abe.

GLOSSARY

As with all fields of human interest there are special words and phrases that we use when talking about the Alexander Technique. Many were put in place by Alexander himself but some have developed over the decades since Alexander's death in 1955, as the users of the Technique have found ways of talking about the Technique that makes sense in modern language.

So here is a list of words and phrases, used by Alexander teachers and students, with a brief pointer to their meaning. To understand the full meaning will often require a commitment to studying the Technique. Fuller explanations are found in the main chapters of the book.

FM We sometimes use Alexander's first two initials to refer to him, and his brother **AR**, who was also involved in teaching the work.

Their given names were Frederick Matthias and Albert Redden.

F M Alexander's four books

MSI *Man's Supreme Inheritance* – Alexander's first book

CCC *Constructive Conscious Control* – Alexander's second book

UOS *The Use of the Self* – Alexander's third book

UCL *The Universal Constant in Living* – Alexander's fourth and final book that looks in detail at his assertion that **use affects functioning**

Various Alexander concepts

Anti-gravity reflex A term used for the person's in-built response to gravity. The reflex that lengthens the spine in response to gravity's downward influence.

Atlanto-occipital joint (AO joint) The joint between the head and the rest of the body, at the top of the spine; the **occiput** is a section of bone at the bottom of the skull, the **atlas** is the top vertebra of the spine.

Deepening Releasing that creates an expansion or more space between the front and back of the body.

Doing End-gaining. Not *allowing* things to happen but *making* them happen. Doing or trying tends to be less efficient, less coordinated.

Downward pull The opposite of lengthening – this is a habit, usually with a negative emotional source. It is created by unnecessary effort or tension pulling the head 'down' or 'back and down' or 'forward in space and down'.

End-gaining When you are more interested in the result or end than the **means-whereby** you might achieve that end. You become an **end-gainer,** in Alexander terms, if you are focused on the goal and not choosing how you do things.

Faulty (unreliable or debauched) sensory awareness
The state of our sensory feedback when we feel we are doing something different to what we are actually doing.

Kinaesthesia Your sense of movement in your body. The sense of acceleration and deceleration in movement.

Lengthening This implies a release of muscles that are unnecessarily tightened. As muscles work less they get longer (and thinner), this takes pressure off the joints, creating more freedom, and allows the body to lengthen. If the extensor muscles are working, they organize the spine into a **lengthening** condition.

Means-whereby The method or way in which you might best achieve your goals.

Narrowing The opposite of widening – muscular tension that is often expressing lack of confidence – it can also be a response to feeling the cold.

Non-doing Choosing your modus operandi with the **means-whereby** in mind. Allowing your unimpaired coordination to work for you. 'Inhibiting' of the habitual modus.
Primary Control The relationship between the head and the spine. It has a global effect on all your activity. We are looking to allow the in-built head-righting reflexes to be active in this relationship.
Proprioception Your sense of position, relative angles and balance within your body.
Psychophysical Unity The concept that the mind and body are one functioning unit not two separable parts.
The Self The whole person, the mind, body, emotions and spirit
Sensory awareness Feedback from your senses of which you are conscious.
Spiralling The concept of turning that includes lengthening.
Use The way you use your mind and body.
Use affects functioning The way you use your mind and body affects the way they function. This is central to the Technique.
Widening This happens when you release muscles that are narrowing your body.

Phrases that refer to applying the principles

Body Mapping A conscious appreciation of your functional anatomy. Barbara and William Conable devised this approach.
Conscious Control Developed awareness of what you are doing that makes choices available and the application of Inhibition and Direction.
Constructive Conscious Control The conscious setting up of a framework of how to work on changes in your life, for example, the recognition of habit, the concepts of Primary Control, Inhibition and Direction.
Direction A willing or wishing of parts of the body to move on a certain journey. The act of 'directing' affects the motor and balancing systems that predispose your body to change in the

desired way. You can also direct your attention, emotions or awareness.

Head forward and up Two Directions relating to the desired tendency in the head's movement; 'forward in this context is a tipping, rotating or rolling forward of the head on the 'atlanto-occipital joint' (see **AO joint**) where your head balances on the top of your spine – *it is not bending the neck forward so the head moves forward in space.* The 'up' element is simple; it is whatever Direction in which your spine is pointing.

Hands-on work The practical, hands on, part of an Alexander lesson or turn.

Inhibition A moment of consciousness before you go into action when you acknowledge to yourself that you have choices. You 'inhibit' or decide to stop negative habitual or automatic behaviour. You can apply Inhibition continuously to avoid a negative habit when you are playing your instrument – it becomes part of your awareness.

Lunge An approach to organizing the transfer of weight on the feet in relation to the hands, arms and back (see figure, p. 168).

Monkey – a position of mechanical advantage Somewhere between standing and sitting or squatting but keeping full stature. A coordinated state that is balancing equally on two feet with released hips, knees and ankles. (See p. 167 for a photo and more detail.)

Opposition in Direction A reference to putting Directions in a larger context. For example, the head moves up as the sitting bones connect with the chair. The hands move away from the back as the back moves away from the hands.

Recognition of habit This is simply what it says on the tin – it is usually referring to identifying negative habits that you will then intend to change.

Saddle work Working on your **Use** with or without a teacher while sitting on a saddle. The horse is usually a wooden construction rather than a live animal. You experience the hip joints and legs free from the weight of the upper body.

Send your head up or Think up! Examples of Direction. You think of your head moving in the Direction your spine is pointing – this encourages a coordinated lengthening of the spine.

Thinking in activity The conscious application of the Alexander principles to any activity.

A Turn When an Alexander teacher works with you for a short time, that is, shorter than a lesson.

Wall work (1) Making use of a wall as a reference of perpendicular flatness in relation to the back of your curved body; (2) making use of a wall as an unmovable flat surface to put hands on while changing position and orientation of your body's weight, Direction and energy.

Wobble board A wobbly platform used to develop more subtle balancing ability.

Work on yourself Personal work, consciously applying the Principles, as you have understood them from lessons or your reading. Your Alexander thinking in practice, performance and everyday life.

Three Alexander 'procedures'

'Hands on the back of a chair' or 'Hands on a chair' or 'HOBC' A procedure, described by **FM** in his second book, *Constructive Conscious Control* (**CCC**). This is a dynamic exercise to improve breathing and connect the hands to the back, preparatory for all manner of activities. The procedure can be performed standing or sitting with a suitable chair in front of you, on which to put your hands (see figure, p. 148).

Semi-supine A position that we choose to adopt to restore coordinated **use**, recharge our batteries and find a neutral state. In an Alexander context, semi-supine implies that you will be thinking Directions while lying down. You lie on your back (on the carpet) with your head on a book and your knees bent, feet reasonably near you on the floor (you can see a photo of someone lying in semi-supine on an Alexander table, p. 131). See Chapter 13 for more detail.

Whispered 'Ah' Another procedure, this one involving the breathing and vocal mechanisms. You 'inhibit, 'direct' and aspirate the ah vowel (the most open vowel sound). See Chapter 10: Breathing, for details of this procedure. Everyone can benefit from this practice as it improves breathing and vocal coordination.

Common health issues for musicians

CTS Carpal tunnel syndrome; this is manifest as reduced capacity in the hand with numbness in the thumb and fingers caused by pressure on the nerve passing through the wrist. Improved use of the hand, wrist and arm, in the context of an overall improvement in **Use** can solve the problem.

Curvature of the spine There are various named distortions of the spine, for example, kyphosis, lordosis and scoliosis. All people are susceptible but these problems can develop for musicians who make less than optimal **Use** of the body to play their instrument.

RSI Repetitive strain injury; a condition suffered by musicians (as well as others) caused by repeated gestures with poorly coordinated **Use.** Application of the Alexander principles alleviates the symptoms as well as being a preventative strategy.

BIBLIOGRAPHY

F. M. Alexander's books

Man's Supreme Inheritance. London: Mouritz, 2002.

Constructive Conscious Control of the Individual. London: Mouritz, 2004.

The Use of the Self. London: Victor Gollancz, 1985.

Universal Constant in Living. London: Mouritz, 2000.

Brown, Ron, *Authorised Summaries of F M Alexander's Four Books*. London: STAT Books, 1992.

Biographies of F. M. Alexander

Bloch, Michael, *The Life of F M Alexander*. London: Time Warner Book Group, 2004.

Evans, J. A., *Frederick Matthias Alexander: A Family History*. West-Sussex: Phillimore & Co, 2001.

Anatomy orientated books

Bond, Mary, *The New Rules of Posture*. Rochester, VT: Healing Arts Press, 2007.

Calsis-Germain, Blandine, *The Anatomy of Movement* (revised edition). Seattle, WA: Eastland Press, 2007.

Conable, Barbara, *What Every Musician Needs to Know About the Body*. Portland: Andover Press, 2000.

Dimon, Theodore, *Anatomy of the Moving Body*. Berkeley, CA: North Atlantic Books, 2008.

— *The Body in Motion: Its Evolution and Design*. Berkeley, CA: North Atlantic Books, 2011.

Franklin, Eric, *Dynamic Alignment through Movement*. Champaign, IL: Human Kinetics, 1996.

Gorman, David, *The Body Moveable*. Guelph, Canada: Ampersand Press, 2002.

Johnson, Jennifer, *What Every Violinist Needs to Know About the Body*. Chicago: Gia Publications, 2009.

Mark, Thomas, *What Every Pianist Needs to Know About the Body*. Chicago: Gia Publications, 2006.

Myers, Thomas, *Anatomy Trains* (second edition). Toronto: Churchill Livingstone, 2009.

Pearson, Lea, *What Every Flautist Needs to Know About the Body*. Chicago: Gia Publications, 2006.

Alexander books related to music

Alcantara, Pedro de, *Indirect Procedures*. Oxford: Oxford University Press, 1997.

— *Integrated Practice*. New York: Oxford University Press, 2011.

Langford, Elisabeth, *Mind and Muscle: An Owners Handbook*. Antwerp: Garant Uitgevers, 1999.

— *Mind Muscle and Music*. Leuven: Alexandertechniquecentrum vzw, 2008.

Mackie, Vivian, *Just Play Naturally*. Bloomington, IN: Xlibris, 2006.

Alexander voice books

McCallion, Michael, *The Voice Book*. Chatham, Kent: Mackays of Chatham, 1998.

Macdonald, Robert, *The Use of the Voice*. London: Macdonald Media, 1997.

McEvenue, Kelly, *The Alexander Technique for Actors*. London: Methuen Drama, 2001.

Murdoch, Ron, *Born to Sing*, ATCN: Mijmegen, 2011.

Theodore, Dimon, *Your Body Your Voice*. Berkeley, CA: North Atlantic Books, 2011.

Turner, J. Clifford and Boston, *Jane, Voice and Speech in the Theatre*. London: Methuen Drama, 2007.

Alexander books (general)

Barlow, Wilfred, *The Alexander Principle*. London: Arrow Books, 1975.

— *More Talk of Alexander*. London: Gollanz, 1978.

Brennan, Richard, *The Alexander Workbook*. Boston: Element Books, 1992.

Carrington, Walter, *Personally Speaking*, Walter Carrington in conversation with Sean Carey. London: Mouritz, 2000.

— *Thinking Aloud, Talks on Teaching the Alexander Technique*, ed. Jerry Sontag. San Francisco: Mornum Time Press, 1994.

Chance, Jeremy, *The Alexander Technique*. London: Thorsons, 1998.

Conable, Barbara, *Marjory Barstow Her Teaching and Training*. Portland: Andover Press, 1998.

Conable, Barbara and William, *How to Learn the Alexander Technique: A Manual for Students*. Portland: Andover Press, 1995.

Dart, Raymond, *Skill and Poise*. London: STAT Books, 1996.

Dimon, Theodore, *The Elements of Skill*. Berkeley, CA: North Atlantic Books, 2003.

Gelb, Michael, *Body Learning*. London: Aurum Press, 1987.

— *How to Think Like Leonardo*. New York: Delacorte Press, 1998.

Gray, John, *Your Guide to the Alexander Technique*. London: Victor Gollanz, 1990.

Jones, Frank Pierce, *Freedom to Change*. London: Mouritz, 1976.

— *Collected Writings on the Alexander* Technique, ed. Theodore Dimon and Richard Brown. Massachusetts: Alexander Technique Archives, 1998.

Leibowitz, Judith and Connington, Bill, *The Alexander Technique* (Cedar edition). London: Hutchinson, 1994.

MacDonald, Glynn, *The Complete Illustrated Guide to the Alexander Technique*. Boston: Element Books, 1998.

Macdonald, Patrick, *The Alexander Technique As I See It*. Brighton: Rahula Books, 1989.

Nettl-Fiol, Rebecca and Vanier, Luc, *Dance and the Alexander Technique*. Urbana-Champaign: University of Illinois Press, 2011.

Nicholls, Carolyn, *Body Breath and Being*. Hove: D & B Publishing, 2008.

Park, Glen, *The Art of Changing*. Bath: Ashgrove Press, 1989.

Shaw, Steven and D'Angour, Armand, *The Art of Swimming*. Bath: Ashgrove, 1998.

Vineyard, Missy, *How You Stand, How You Move, How You Live*. New York: Marlowe and Company, 2007.

Other related books

Bates, W. H., *The Cure of Imperfect Sight*. New York: Central Fixation, 2011.

Baulk, Malcolm and Shields, Andrew, *Master the Art of Running*. London: Collins and Brown, 2006.

Benjamin, Harry, *Better Sight Without Glasses*. Wellingborough: Thorsons, 1974.

Coyle, Daniel, *The Talent Code*. London: Arrow Books, 2010.

Fehumi, Les and Robbins, Jim, *The Open Focus Brain*. Boston: Trumpeter Books, 2007.

Gallwey, Timothy and Green, Barry, *The Inner Game of Music*. London: Pan Books, 1987.

Grunwald, Peter, *Eyebody*. Auckland: Eyebody Press, 2004.

Tai Chi type books

Chen Man-ch'ing, *Tai Chi Ch'uan*. Berkeley, CA: North Atlantic Books, 1981.

Hanson, Rick, *Buddah Brain*. Oakland: New Harbinger, 2009.

USEFUL WEBSITES AND CONTACTS

Our website: www.alexandernow.org

Alexander societies

Australia: www.austat.org.au
Belgium: www.fmalexandertec.be
Brazil: www.abtalexander.com.br
Canada: www.canstat.ca
Denmark: www.dflat.dk
Finland: www.finstat.fi
France: www.techniquealexander.info
Germany: www.alexander-technik.org
Israel: www.alexander.org.il
Japan: www.jastat.jp
The Netherlands: www.alexandertechniek.nl
New Zealand: www.alexandertechnique.org.nz
Norway: www.alexanderteknikk.no
South Africa: www.alexandertechnique.org.za
Spain: www.apgae.net
Switzerland: www.alexandertecnik.ch
UK: www.stat.org.uk
USA: www.amstatonline.org

Music/Alexander sites

Body Mapping: www.bodymap.org
Pedro de Alcantara: www.pedrodealcantara.com
Selma Goken: www.welltemperedmusician.com

Tonalis: www.tonalismusic.co.uk
The Violinist in Balance: www.violinistinbalance.nl
More links: www.alexandertechnique.com/musicians.htm

Other Alexander sites

Alexander blog feed: http://alextech.wikia.com/wiki/AT_Blog_Feed
Alexander books: www.ati-net.com/orderinf.php
Alexander Technique International: www.ati-net.com
Direction magazine: www.directionjournal.com
Friends of the Alexander Technique: www.atfriends.org
HITE London: www.hiteltd.co.uk/international
Jessica Wolf's *The Art of Breathing*: http://theartofbreathing.net/stough_institute.html
More books: www.alexanderbooks.co.uk/books.php?MEDIA=Book
Mouritz books: www.mouritz.co.uk
Robert Rickover: www.alexandertechniquenebraska.com
Theodore Dimon books: www.dimoninstitute.org/books